W9-BYV-334

A Garland Series

The English Stage
Attack and Defense 1577 - 1730

A collection of 90 important works
reprinted in photo-facsimile in 50 volumes

edited by
Arthur Freeman
Boston University

Heydegger's Letter
to the Bishop of London

John James Heidegger

A Seasonable Apology
for Mr. H—g—r

P.W.

The Conduct of the Stage Considered

with a preface
for the Garland Edition by

Arthur Freeman

Garland Publishing, Inc., New York & London

1973

Library of Congress Cataloging in Publication Data

Heidegger, John James, 1659?-1748.
　Heydegger's letter to the Bishop of London.

　(The English stage: attack and defense, 1577-1730)
　Reprint of 3 works, the 1st originally printed in
1724 for N. Cox, London; the 2d originally printed in
1724 for A. Moor, London; and the 3d originally printed
in 1721 for E. Matthews, London.
　1.　Theater—Moral and religious aspects.
I.　A seasonable apology for Mr. H—g—r.　1973.
II.　The conduct of the stage considered.　1973.
III.　Title.　IV.　Series.
PN2047.H35　　792'.013　　72-170487
ISBN 0-8240-0628-3

Preface

*John James Heidegger (?1659-1749) was in part
responsible for the importation of Italian opera
into England, and as manager of the Haymarket
opera house, with the long collaboration of
Handel, raised the new genre to be the rage of
play-going London, assumed the Mastership of the
Revels, and long dominated, with wit, opulence,
and to his own great personal profit, a good
portion of the London stage from c. 1720 to 1738.
He was almost mythically ugly, and remarkably
cheerful about it, his extraordinary countenance
being celebrated by Pope, Fielding, and Chester-
field in prose, and by Hogarth in several prints.
Some documents relating to his career are re-
produced by Nichol,* History of English Drama,
1660-1900 *(1952), II,* ad loc.

*Heidegger's introduction of masquerades into his
operas (c. 1717) at Haymarket provoked a storm
of surprisingly vehement protest, some of it
certainly from jealous rivals. A Royal Proclamation
at one time forbade them, whereupon their name
was simply changed to "ridottos" or "balls," and*

5

PREFACE

even George II continued to be seen, uncon-cernedly, in attendance. But there were severe hearings by a Middlesex Grand Jury, and the Bishop of London preached against Heidegger's masquerades in 1724, calling forth this brief retort in verse (Lowe-Arnott-Robinson 356), which we reprint from a copy in the British Museum (11631.k.6; reduced), collating A-B². And a sup-plementary apology of the same year (Lowe-Arnott-Robinson 357) adduced scriptural prece-dents as well; the dedication is signed "P.W." We reprint the British Museum copy (641.e.48), col-lating $A^3 B-D^4 E^1 (=A4?)$.*

The Conduct of the Stage Consider'd *treats especially of the "pernicious consequences of masquerades," and is perhaps typical of the opposition's attitude, when formulated as prin-ciple. Rather a monotonous and workaday retailing of stale arguments out of Biblical and classical authority, it has been attributed for no obvious reason to Charles Owen (d. 1746), the dissenting presbyterian. We reprint the British Museum copy (641.e.47), collating $A-E^4 F^2$ (Lowe-Arnott-Robinson 355).*

May, 1973 A.F.

6

HEYDEGGER's

LETTER

TO THE

Bishop of *LONDON.*

Qui nos damnant, sunt Histriones maximi ; i. e.
They that damn *Masquerades*, will go to a *Hop.*

LONDON:

Printed for N. Cox in *Story's-Passage,* going out of *St. James's-Park.*
M DCC XXIV.   *Price 6 d.*

HEYDEGGER's

LETTER

TO THE

Bishop of *L O N D O N.*

My L O R D,

Y O U R Sermon, preach'd at *Bow,*
Came to my Hands some Weeks ago.
By which I find you seem afraid,
That harmless Pastime, MASQUERADE,
May spoil the *Reformation Trade.*

With

With kind Concern and Pious Zeal,
In Strains Prophetick, you foretel,
What fad Difafters muft betide
The Wives and Daughters of *Cheapfide*,
If mixing with the Courtly-Crowd,
They wear Difguifes *a-la-mode*:
And, if I underftand your Speeches,
No City Dame fhou'd wear the Breeches.

I HOPE, my Lord, you'll pardon me,
If in fome Points we difagree.

'TIS Prudence to fupply with Art,
Where Nature fails to do her Part:
When borrow'd Looks give lefs Offence,
To ufe one's own is Impudence.

THE World it felf, excufe the Phrafe, is
A Ball; where, mimick Shapes and Faces,
The Judgment of our Senfes cheat,
And Fafhion favours the Deceit:

Where

Where from *Fifteen* to *Sixty Three*,
Fond of diffembling, *all* agree
In one continu'd *Mummery*

Joiners fometimes have pafs'd for *Princes*,
Fidlers have made the fame Pretences:
This Ifle, as well as *Spain*, has feen
A *Monk* affume a *Monarch*'s Mein. *
And once his HOLINESS, You know,
Was but a WHORE *incognito*.
Oft has a *Garter* and a *Star*
Conceal'd a furly fawcy *Tar:*
Many, mifled by Shews, mifcall
A *Butcher* Captain-General.
Thus *Scriv'ners* feem *Prime-Minifters*,
And *Oyfter-Women, Barrifters:*
A *Juggler*, hid by *hallow'd Beaver*,
May ape an *Orthodox Believer*;
And fure it will be no hard Task,
To prove a M—e is a Mask.

* *See the following Account of Don Ramiro, &c.*　† *Pope Joan.*

THEN,

THEN, good my Lord of *L----n*, why
In this mad Age, ſhould *You* and *I*
Diſpute, ſince 'tis ſo neceſſary
To change our *Forms*, and *Habits* vary?
Better for *both*, with honeſt Rage,
Like brave *Don Quixot*, to engage
The darling *Windmill* of the Stage ; *
Teach the *Beau Monde* to be leſs civil
To their old Enemy the *Devil.* †

WHEN theſe *dull licens'd Follies* fail
To pleaſe, *Good Manners* muſt prevail;
Virtue will ſoon want no *Defenſe*;
For *ſhameleſs Vice* is Want of *Senſe.*

HAY-MARKET,
Eaſter-Monday, 1724.   HEYDEGGER.

---

* Rich's *Necromancer*: *Or*, Harlequin *Doctor* Fauſtus.   † Ibid.

SOME
ACCOUNT
OF
Don *RAMIRO*, King of ARAGON.

Qui capit, ille facit.

N the Year of our Lord 1137 Don *Ramiro* II. King of *Aragon*, who, after the Death of his Brother Don *Alphonso* I. (who became King of *Leon* and *Castile* by his Marriage with the celebrated Donna *Urraca*, Heirefs to thofe Realms, famous for her Gallantries,) was taken out of his Cell in the Abbey of St. *Ponce*, and fet upon the Throne. In a *Spanish* Book, written by *Jorge de Monte-Mayor*, concerning this Monkifh King Don *Ramiro*, I met with a remarkable Story. Having been from his Youth bred up in a Monaftick Life, he would not have quitted it for the Throne, had he not been abfolutely commanded fo to do by the Pope. The States of *Aragon* obliged him to marry, and he began to reign with great Lenity and religious Simplicity. Several of the Grandees of that Realm obferving his Eafinefs, had him in Contempt, and had the Infolence to make him divers out-of-the-way Propofals, and to give him fome very ridiculous Counfel. Among other Things, being upon taking the Field, in order to oppofe an Army of *Moors*, who had invaded his Dominions, fome of thofe fneering Sycophants advifed him to march out of his Capital City *Saragofa*, Sword in Hand. He did fo, but found himfelf fo embarafs'd with his Sword and Shield, both his Hands being employ'd, that he was at an utter Lofs what to do with his Bridle. Upon this he asked them, *How he fhould hold his Horfe's Reins?* They anfwered him, *Your Majefty muft hold them with your Teeth.* He innocently did fo. But another of the Grandees, who had a true Veneration for that Prince, obferving how he was impos'd upon, undeceiv'd him, and gave him to underftand that he had been abus'd. Don *Ramiro*, tho' fitter for a Convent than a Throne, did not want Senfe, and fufficiently refented the Affront he perceived had been put upon him by his prefumptious Subjects; and no fooner alighted from his Horfe, but he wrote to a certain antient Monk, who had been his Tutor in the Monaftery where he had refided, to ask his Advice what to do in that Cafe, and gave the Letter into the Hands of that loyal Courtier, who had difabus'd him. That Nobleman immediately departed; and coming to the Convent, delivered the Letter as directed. Being introduc'd, he was conducted into the Garden, where he found the venerable Reclufe very ferioufly walking; who having read the Letter, drew out a Pair of Sciffars, and began to fnip off the Heads of the talleft Flowers. The Nobleman perceiving that he made no Hafte to difpatch him, faid, *Be pleafed to confider, Father, that his Majefty order'd me to return with all poffible Speed.* The Monk replied, *Your Lordfhip may return as foon as you pleafe, for I have nothing to fay to your Letter.* But the Grandee importuning him to give him at leaft fome Token, whereby

whereby the King might be certified that he had done his Errand, the holy Man only faid, *You may tell his Majefty all you have feen and heard. I have no more to fay to him at prefent.* The Nobleman finding it in vain to importune him any longer, returned to Court; where he gave an Account to Don *Ramiro* of what happened. That Prince, who readily took the Hint, immediately iffued out an Order to fummon all the Grandees of the Realm to Court, having, as he gave out, Matters of the greateft Importance to communicate to them. They came; and the King faid, *My Lords, I have fent for you to ask your Advice : I have had it in my Head for fome Time to make a* BELL, *that may be heard not only throughout my own Dominions, but likewife in thofe of my Neighbour's. How fhall I manage it?* Thofe who had play'd upon him before, imagining this to be one of Don *Ramiro's* Simplicities, to'd him fmiling, That an Affair of fo extraordinary a Nature would require fome Confideration, and demanded a Month's Time : He granted it, with Orders, that, the Month. being expir'd, they fhould not fail to return with their Anfwer. At the Time prefix'd they all came, except thofe who truly refpected the King, who chofe rather to undergo the Cenfure of Difobedience, than to be prefent at the difrefpectful Treatment they were perfuaded their Soveraign would meet with from his fneering Grandees. The King upon that Day apparell'd himfelf in all his *Regalia,* and had moft magnificently adorned a fpacious Hall, the Tapeftry whereof he had order'd to be hung at fome Diftance from the Walls, and that his Body Guards, armed at all Points, fhould be pofted round the Apartment, concealed behind the Hangings. The Grandees being come, they began to utter feveral ridiculous Extravagancies relating to the Advice he had asked of them about the *Bell.* Don *Ramiro,* incens'd at their Infolence, gave the Signal, the Hangings were let fall in an Inftant, and the Guard appeared all in Arms. Then advanced four Executioners, and as many Friars; and the King, with a ftern Countenance, and angry Tone, faid, *To the Intent that thofe who ferve a mild Prince, may learn how to deport themfelves with due Refpect towards him, I propos'd to you the making a Bell, which might be heard is ours and the neighbouring States : This Bell is no other than your Heads, which, as Traytors to your Soveraign, fhall be now fever'd from your Bodies.* They, in a Confternation, would have excufed themfelves; but the King would hear nothing, and they were all immediately executed in his Prefence. The Heads were placed in a Ring round a Table, and that of the principal Perfon among them, in the Middle, and a large Carpet thrown over them. Their Sons were prefently fent for to Court, to whom the King faid, *You here behold the Heads of your Fathers, which for their having fail'd in their Refpect to me their Soveraign, I have caufed to be feparated from their Bodies : Take Warning by this Example, and learn to behave your felves better than they have done. Their Eftates, Titles, and Dignities I beftow upon you; live and enjoy them : But never let the Sound of this Bell be out of your Ears.* After this the King was refpected and obeyed by all his Subjects. It alfo became a Proverb throughout *Spain,* (when any one was turbulent,) *Haze mas Ruydo que la* Campana de Aragon; *He makes more Noife than the* Bell *of* Aragon.

THERE were other Kings in *Spain* who had been *Monks,* and in particular Don *Alphonfo* IV. King of *Leon* and *Caftile,* who, in the Year 924, ambitious of a Crown, left his Cell to afcend the Throne; but after a troublefome Reign of fix or feven Years, he was again fhut up in his Monaftery by his Brother Don *Ramiro* II. and fome fay that he deprived him of his Sight.

F I N I S.

A Seasonable

APOLOGY

FOR

Mr. ~~Heidegger~~.

Proving the Usefulness and
Antiquity of Masquerading from
Scripture, and prophane History.

WITH

OBSERVATIONS on the several Species
of MASKS now in Use:

AND LIKEWISE

The Report from the Committee appointed to state and examine the Advantages arising from our present
Masquerades.

LONDON:

Printed for *A. Moor*, near St. Paul's. 1724.
Price Six-pence. *June.*

To that moſt Celebrated

MATRON, diſguiſs'd and diſtin-
guiſh'd by the Name and Title of
Mother N———m.

MADAM,

OU are ſenſible it has been
cuſtomary for Writers in all
Ages, at leaſt ſuch as expeꝃ-
ed Immortality, to prefix the
Name of ſome extraordinary
Perſon to other Labours, to give them
Countenance and Proteꝃion; and that it
was poſſible, after I had undertaken an
Apology for Mr. H———r, and Defence
of the Uſefulneſs of Maſquerades, I could
be at a Loſs for a Patroneſs, whilſt ſo
great an Encourager of the Liberal Arts
and Sciences was in Being as Yourſelf.
The Cauſes, Courſes and Conſequences of
theſe Entertainments, naturally led me to
you for Proteꝃion, becauſe only one of your
Calling

The DEDICATION.

Calling was proper to my Purpose. Tho' it's true, indeed, had I been a vain Person, that had affected the Reputation of being either acquainted with, or beholden to the Quality, I might have found out some one in a higher Class, to have address'd my self to on this Occasion. But as I had chosen a most useful Subject, so I was not weak enough to choose a less useful Patroness; for no Body at this Time of the Day carries on such a Stroke of Business as you do.

A Masquerade is so properly yours, and so much your Concern, that if it is not your own Child, 'tis really your Nursery; and whatever the Motives may be of those Entertainments, 'tis certain, that the House you keep with unrival'd Reputation, is the real Scene of Action; and to you, as it is with some others in a less Degree, that these Masquerades owe the Opportunity of the finishing Stroke and Consummation of the Business. So that notwithstanding I have prov'd in the following Treatise, beyond Contradiction, the important Uses of Masquerades; yet I am here bound to acknowledge, that at your House chiefly, it is, that those very Uses are apply'd; so that I think, I may modestly assure my self of your motherly Protection; as not only your own Interest is concern'd in it, but likewise, that

the

the common Method of carrying on your
own Bufinefs feparate from this, is wholly
in Mafquerade; unlefs it is when fome of
your Nymphs are fo obliging to appear
quite naked. It is to the Mafk of Sanctity,
fac'd with the Practice of Piety, and fome
other Books properly chofen, that you can
cover the Lewdnefs you get a Livelihood
by: It is to the Mafks of artificial Maiden-
heads, that you get a good Price for Girls
that have been us'd before : It is likewife,
to a little Machine, or mafking Habit,
which fhall be Namelefs, that you preferve one Child from the Infection of another; the Clothes too, from the Tally-Man,
Mafks the Nakednefs of your Nymphs, to
make 'em pafs current; and your Paint
and Wafhes difguife their Complexions:
They too, with Honey in their Mouths, are
oftentimes found to have Stings in their
Tails: So that after ftating the Cafe fo
exactly betwixt you and my felf, I think
it is as reafonable for me to expect your
Protection, as 'tis for you to expect to
Thrive by your Calling; for one Thing I
am fure of, that fcarce a Mafquerade has
been, but in Confequence of it, you have
had the Entertainment of near one hundred Couples of Mafqueraders; who, when
they had chang'd their Moneys, doubtlefs
pay'd you fufficiently for your Time and
Trouble,

The DEDICATION.

Trouble, and as some of these were People of the best Quality, so your Interest will certainly be sufficient for me, and my Client too, and your Protection will eternally oblige

Madam,

Your most dutiful Son

and Servant

P. W.

A Seaſonable

APOLOGY

FOR

Mr. *H—g—r*.

Proving the Uſefulneſs and
Antiquity of Maſquerading from Scripture, and prophane Hiſtory.

 Am ſenſible that in writing an Apology for this Gentleman, I ſhall encounter with Prejudices ſufficient to deter any Pen, leſs daring than mine, from the Attempt, and rouſe up ſo many different Parties to oppoſe me, that were not the Ladies my good and faithful Allies, I ſhould deſpair of Succeſs.

B

But

But infpir'd with Charms which I can no longer refift, and fupported by Facts that no reafonable Man can conteft, I here enter the Lifts as their Champion, and throw down my Gauntlet in Defiance of the boldeft of my Oppofers.

I take it for granted, that in Cafe I prove the Ufefulnefs and Antiquity of Mafquerading, I fhall go a great Way towards the Vindication of my Client, and as I proceed too, fhall anfwer the Reflections his Enemies have thrown upon him, and make it appear how neceffary fuch an extraordinary Genius is at this Juncture.

And firft to prove the Ufefulnefs of Mafquerading from Scripture, I fhall Inftance the Fall of our firft Parents : *Adam* and *Eve* fo lately form'd by the Wifdom and Power of Almighty God, had fuch a Meafure of Purity and Perfection, as fufficiently qualified them to withftand all the Affaults they were liable to ; and the Devil, with all his Power and Malice, could not hope to compafs his Ends by Force, and therefore neceffarily had Recourfe to Fraud : But to come to enfnare them with Fallacies in any Appearance fuitable to the Greatnefs proper to himfelf, his fubtilty well knew, would foon alarm their
Virtue,

Virtue, and put them upon their Guard;
and therefore cunningly chofe the Mafk
of a Serpent, (an abject infignificant
Creature, and at that Time harmlefs) to
execute his Purpofes; in which he fuc-
ceeded, to defpoil them, and all their
Pofterity, of their Innocence and Perfection. And pardon me, courteous Reader, if I exult a little in the modeft
Affurance I have of gaining a compleat
Victory; having already produc'd fuch
a notorious Fact in Behalf of my Client; and let me defy too, any one that
has any Faith in reveal'd Religion, to
contradict me, if I affert, that it proves
the Ufefulnefs of Mafquerading with
a Vengeance. How hard is it then, that
my Client fhould be reproach'd any
longer with promoting Entertainments
void of Ufefulnefs or Defign; when I
have, and fhall fully make it appear in
the Courfe of my Arguments, as well as
from his own Succeffes, how exactly he
falls in with the Tafte and Genius of
of the *Britifh* Nation. We are, properly
fpeaking, an Ifland full of Politicians,
for our very Women and Children dab-
ble in Politicks, and fuch of our Clergy as are confcious they underftand not
Divinity, fupply that Defect, with Po-
litical Sermons; and find their Account
in it too, if they happen but luckily

to be on the wrong Side of the Que-
ftion: Now, my Client, (that even
fucceeding Generations may confefs
his Ufefulnefs) having confider'd how
difficult it is to underftand aright the
Maxims of *Machiavel*, and that few have
either Leifure or Capacity for the Tafk ;
and to encourage fome enterprifing
young Gentlemen, that would gladly,
without the Pains of thinking, be
thought wifer than their Neighbours,
and expect fome Time or other, to
lord it over their Betters, has cook'd
up an Entertainment, call'd a Mafquerade, where even the moft refin'd Politicks of the infernal Cabinet are re-
duc'd to Practice, and made eafy to
the meaneft Capacity. Now, as the
Devil is indifputably the profoundeft
Politician, and ufes Mafks in his greateft Enterprizes, and my Client is allow'd to have the beft Genius for con-
triving a Mafquerade ; fo, the many and
wonderful Things that have been tranfacted at fome of them, fufficiently confirm their Ufefulnefs.

The fecond Fact I fhall recite from
Scripture, to prove the Ufefulnefs of
Mafquerading, is the Story of *Lot* and
his two Daughters ; *Lot*, though a juft
Man, and lately efcap'd from the Ruin
that overthrew *Sodom* and *Gomorrah*, had
his

his Virtue fapp'd by the Force of a Mafk, (for Drunkennefs is a Difguife, and a Diguife is a Mafk) and committed Inceft with his Daughters. The Girls it feems, being in a defolate Place, where Men were fcarce, refolv'd however, not to lofe their Teeming-Time, but to trick even their own Father into the Bufinefs ; nor were they long at a Lofs how·to undermine his Virtue by the Force of a Difguife, having been bred in *Sodom*, which, in the modern Senfe, was a very polite Place, and as fuch, neceffarily had its Mafquerades ; and to the Succeffion of thefe inceftuous Enterprizes, was owing thofe two great Nations of *Moab* and *Ammon*. *Thamar* too, the Daughter-in-law of *Judah*, who had been abus'd by the Impiety of *Err* and *Onan*, and, to her Prejudice, remain'd ftill a Widow in her Father *Judah*'s Houfe, notwithftanding his youngeft Son was now grown up to Years of Maturity ; in the Mafk of an Harlot, tricks that Prince and Patriarch, to commit Inceft with her, by which Encounter fhe had Iffue ; the Want of which was a heavy Reproach amongft the *Ifraelites*. And fure I am, that I may modeftly claim a good deal of Merit of this Kind for my Client ; fince fuch Numbers of wealthy People, that

had

had long lamented the Want of Heirs, now tranſported, behold their Nurſeries ſtock'd with Children ; for Impotency on the Man's Side, is hardly a Misfortune, where the Wife has the free Uſe of Maſquerades ; and how comfortable muſt it needs be, to a Gentleman that labours under ſuch a Defect, to ſee with what Alacrity his good Lady ſhall repair to theſe Entertainments, in order to ſupply it.

I might inſtance too here, by the Help of a Maſk *Jacob* obtain'd the Bleſſing from his Father *Iſaac* ; but that being a Uſe not intended by my Client, I ſhall wave it. And how *Micab* too, the Daughter of *Saul*, ſav'd her Huſband *David*, by impoſing an Image, dreſs'd and laid to Bed in his Stead, on the Meſſengers of *Saul*, 'till he was eſcap'd out of their Reach : But this being foreign likewiſe to the Deſign of my Client, I ſhall drop it with the other, tho' both of them ſerve to prove the Point in Hand ; and taking my Leave of Sacred Writ, which has abundantly prov'd the Uſefulneſs of Maſquerading, I ſhall paſs on to prophane Hiſtory.

It would be endleſs to recite the Adventures of the Heathen Deities, who are repreſented by the Poets to have

have been perpetually in Mafquerade ; efpecially when a Rape, or any fuch momentous Affair was to be tranfacted : The old Thunderer himfelf, has, according to them, varied his Difguifes, as often as é'er *Proteus* did his Shape, and always found it fubfervient to his Defigns. But preferring the Gravity of Hiftory to the Fiction of Poets, I fhall mention that matchlefs Mafquerade at the Siege of *Troy.*

The *Greeks* had for many Years befieg'd that City, and found all their Efforts but of little Effect, at leaft not fufficient to reduce it ; fo that wearied out with ftorming, they had Recourfe to a Mafquerade. A Horfe of an enormous Size, was built, and the Belly of it was ftor'd with armed Men, which the cheated *Trojans* themfelves, drew within their own Walls ; but fo foon as thofe conceal'd in the Mafk, found a proper Opportunity, they iffu'd out, and open'd the Gates to their Friends, who inftantly ravag'd and burnt the proud City to the Ground.

I might come nearer Home too, and mention the *Spanifh* Mafquerade in Queen *Elizabeth*'s Reign, ftiled the *Invincible Armado* ; and doubtlefs it had been found fo, but that the *Englifh* prov- ed the better Mafqueraders. But left I
fhould

should startle some of my unwary Readers by calling it a Masquerade, I will, for their Satisfaction, explain myself as follows : A Ship is most certainly a Mask, and a Man of War the most excellent of the Specie ; and if so, then such a prodigious Fleet, and so well mann'd as theirs was, must certainly have been a very formidable Masquerade, without which Masks of theirs, (as we are an Island) they could never have invaded us.　　As *Waller* says,

Tis not so hard for greedy Foes to spoil
Another Nation, as to touch our Soil.

The same Poet too, speaking of our Situation in another Place, and the Prowess of our Naval Masks in his Time, has it thus:

Angels, and we, have this Prerogative,
That none can at our happy Seats arrive :
Whilst we descend at Pleasure to invade
The Bad, with Vengeance, and the Good,
　　　　　　　　　　(to aid.

But at that Time they were superiour to us, both in Number and Force ; and had not Sir *Francis Drake*, by some new invented Masks, since call'd Fireships, ruin'd their hellish Enterprise,
we

we had undoubtedly *fallen a Prey to their Teeth :* But I have ventur'd on the Recital of this laft Fact without any Inftruction from my Client, who afpires not to the Care of the Commonwealth, being well enough fatisfy'd with the Poft he enjoys at prefent. And therefore modeftly thinks its Safety none of his Bufinefs.

The *Gun-Powder Plot* was a Mafquerade of that unfpeakable Ufefulnefs to the Papifts, and their Caufe, that had it not been difcover'd and prevented, it would infallibly have deftroy'd at one Blow, the whole Legiflature of this Kingdom.

The Mafquerade at *Paris,* commonly call'd the Maffacre, was of that extream Ufe to the Projectors of it, that in one Night, it deftroy'd 100,000 Proteftants. The Mafk was remarkably ufeful to the Regicide that cut off King *Charles*'s Head; it being the Opinion of moft People, that had fuch a Machine been wanting, no one had even at that Time of Madnefs, been defperate enough to have undertaken it; and how effectually it fcreen'd him from Punifhment afterwards, is notorious; for had he been known at the Reftoration, he had certainly fuffer'd

C the

the sharpest Pains that could have been inflicted.

And in our Days how extreamly useful has the Mask been to the Blacks of *Waltham*, insomuch that our Legislature has found itself under a Necessity of making a new Law on Purpose to extirpate them.

O Mask! Great has been at all Times thy Usefulness, and greatly art thou still in Use: By thee fell our first Parents, and by thee Sin and Death enter'd into the World : By thee, *Lot* and *Judah* committed Incest with their own Daughters, and by thee the *Grecians* conquer'd the City of *Troy* : By thee, Sons aspire to the Wombs from whence they sprung, and Daughters wantonly embrace the Loyns that begot them : By thee, Great Ladies talk Bawdy without blushing and envy our Oyster-Women no longer : By thee too, my Client gets Yearly his Thousands, and keeps Mistresses he cannot enjoy.

But I shall now proceed to give further Proofs of the Usefulness of Masquerading from common Sense, and Experience ; and after that is done, if any one shall continue to think evil of my Client, why let the Sin of it rest upon his own Head ; for my own Part, I shall sit down and indulge the Peace and
Quiet

Quiet arising from a good Conscience,
having faithfully discharg'd the Truft
that was repos'd in me.

And that Mafks are extreamly ufeful to almoft all Sorts and Degrees of
People, we know from daily Experience: It is to the Mask of Religion, that
the Hypocrite owes his good Name;
and to the Mask of Honefty, that the
Knave draws well meaning People into
his Clutches in order to cozen them.
It is through the Mask of Bravery, that
the Coward is fuffer'd to be faucy; and
through the Mask of Demureness, that
the Whore gets fometimes a new Spark
at a Chriftening. *The Devil* (we read)
*can transform himself into an Angel of
Light*; and my Client, tho' he once won
a Bett of five Guineas on being found
uglier than *Granny* of frightful Memo-
ry, yet at one of our Mafquerades, I
am told, pafs'd on I———a for the
D—— of P———— till his Impotency
made the Difcovery. But as Things, rather than Perfons, fhould determine us
in our Opinions; fo I fhall affert, that
Religion itfelf, not only ferves to cloak
a World of Wickednefs; but in fome
Ch——hes muft appear in a certain pre-
fcrib'd Drefs; tho in Fact, Religion,
like Truth, is feldom real, and never
can be aimable, unlefs it free from Difguife.

good Set of Masks, and wearing them
properly, is the Excellence: Like a
Story I have heard of a defunct Attor-
ney, one praising of him for having
been excellent in his Way, was answer-
ed by a Brother of the Quill, that indeed he had a good Set of Evidences,
and knew how to fort them to the Cause.
Law, though the Path of Justice, and
Boundary of every Man's Right and
Property, very often serves for a Mask
to the greatest Rapine and Oppression.
Justice herself, the very Soul of this
Gigantick Body, is necessarily painted
blind, for could her Ladyship see as
well as some of her Children can feel,
she would be sometimes in Danger of
Partiallity. To mask Cruelty and Oppression, and skreen it from Justice, is
an Excellency that not only acquires
Reputation to those possess'd of so much
Artfulness, but Estates too, to themselves and Families; and without such
Disguises, there would not, God knows,
be Bread for the tenth Part of the Number that now live in Splendour and
Luxury by it.

Physick is an exact Masquerade, for
after its Professors have, with Study and
Diligence, acquired a competent Knowledge in it, they industriously conceal
the Mystery from other People: Their
Pre-

Prescriptions can only be read by themselves, and their Medicines are all dif-
guis'd; the very Patient himself, tho
he conftantly difburfes the expected
Fee, is entirely in the Dark whether his
Life or Death is the Purchace of it.

Some fell by Laudanum, *and some by* Steel,
And Death in Ambush lay, in every Pill.

Garth's Difpen.

Every Medicine they give, has its
proper Vehicle, as the Bolus its leaf
Gold, the Pill its Wafer, &c. And indeed, 'tis neceffary they fhould give the
nafty Things they prepare, in Mafquerade or, I believe, their Patients would
be as unwilling to take Phyfick, as they
are themfelves.

Poetry is doubtlefs in Mafquerade, for
its Satyr fmiles in your Face, at the
very Time 'tis making you eternally
ridiculous; and all its Inftructions and
Morals are couch'd under Fables, Alle-
gories, Similies, &c.

Its Profeffors too, are commonly in
Mafquerade, for their Appearance is
poor, whilft their Minds are rich beyond Expreffion. Give one of the infpir'd Train a good Theme, or a lucky
Thought, and he fhall in Raptures, tram-
ple on Crowns and Sceptres, tho' he's
fure

fure to get little by it, when touch'd up to an Entertainment, or has not even Bread to fuftain Nature withal, whilft he's working it.

War is likewife a Mafquerade; for firft the Pretence for waging it, is commonly foreign to the real Motives of it, and the Methods of carrying it on, are little elfe but Mafks and Difguifes of the real Defign; or what is marching and countermarching, mining, fapping, Ambufhments, and the like; which are all extremely Ufeful in the Art of War, and neceffary Parts of a Military Mafquerade. Tho', I can't but think, notwithftanding the Cry of Modern Improvements, that our Anceftors had fome Advantages of us in this Art; and it does my Heart good to read fometimes, how fome of thofe ancient Heroes have blufter'd, when fecurely rivited in Iron and Steel; for 'twas eafy for them to be Intrepid, whofe Armour was Cafeharden'd and Weapon Proof; and in Cafe of any new War, I fhould think this Sort of Armour might ftill be convenient to indulge fome young Gentlemen that could not fell out, having never been flufh'd with Victory, nor even feen the Face of an Enemy.

Trade too, is extremely beholden to Mafks, whether Foreign or Domeftick; the Merchant enters one Comodity in
the

the Name of another that pays lefs Duty; and Goods for Exportation, which
he, in his own Confcience knows is for
Home Confumption, and fo fecures the
Drawback, thefe Things being fhipp'd,
but to be run again; the Shopkeeper of
all Kinds, has his Mafk and Myftery, by
which, he receives Sums of Money with
a Servant, as an Aprentice, to do his Bufinefs for him; when otherwife, he
would be Money out of Pocket yearly
to Labourers for doing the fame Bufinefs: The Mechanick too, has his Craft,
which ferves him to the fame Purpofe,
and all thefe Mafks are very ufeful to
their Owners, and without which, the
trading Part could never arife to fuch
Eftates and Honours as they do.

Sport is almoft of all Kinds perform'd
in Mafquerade, the Fifherman's Net has
its Bait, and the Angler's Hook muft
be mafk'd with a Bait, or, I believe, all
will agree with me, 'twould be but in
vain to hope for Fifh. The Fowler is
conceal'd behind his ftalking Horfe, and
the fetting Dog engages the Attention
of the Covey, 'till the Net is drawn o-
ver them, or the fatal Shot is fent a-
mongft them. It is to the Decoys and
Decoy-ducks that we owe the Plenty
we are ferv'd with of that Fowl in
their Seafon, and to Traps and Gins

D   that

that we deftroy Vermine. The Mafk of
Loyalty is very ufeful to thofe that
take the Oaths to the Government, and
mean the Pretender, as it faves them the
Payment of double Taxes. So that to
deny the Ufefulnefs of Mafquerading,
after all that I have urg'd in its Defence,
is, willfully to fhut ones Eyes that one
may not fee.

As to the Antiquity of Mafquerading, the fecond Thing propos'd in my
Title Page, I fhall expect but little Op-
pofition in the Proof of that, unlefs it
be from the Free Mafons, they indeed,
pretend to a great Antiquity ; but without any other Proof than their honeft
Word ; fome of them challenge their
Original from *Solomon*, and fay, they
were Inftituted at the Building of the
firft Temple at *Jerufalem* ; but had the
wifeft of Men been their Inftitutor, they
would then no Doubt have had fome
Secrets worth the betraying long before this Time. Some of this Frater-
nity date their Confufion from the
Tower of *Babel*'s Building ; and one, to
pin the Bafket, that their Antiquity
may be matchlefs, as their Extravagance
is boundlefs, has father'd the Follies of
his Society on the All-wife Creator of
all Things, and calls him their firft
Grand Mafter, as he created the Stru-
ᆴure

&ure of the Univerſe; which Madneſs,
I ſhall not think worth my Trouble of
anſwering, nor tell him, that Matter
was in ſome Senſe in Maſquerade, even
in *Chaos*, being then (as we read) without Form; but ſhall return to the firſt
Fact I recited from Scripture, to prove
the Uſefulneſs of Maſquerades, which
was the Fall of our firſt Parents, ſoon
after the Being of Time, and as ſuch,
ſufficiently enables me to triumph over
theſe wretched Triflers, and aver, that
the Antiquity of Maſquerading is un-
equall'd; and they may, for what I care,
continue ſtill to admit People into Secrets which they will be ſure ſtill to
keep, becauſe out of nothing can nothing
be divulged.

As to the Reflections that have been
thrown upon my Client, they are either
ſo frivolous or ſcurrilous as not to de-
ſerve an Anſwer; however, that I may
not leave any Stone unturn'd that may
be of Service to my Client, I ſhall give
them my Reader, with ſuitable An-
ſwers to them, as follows:

The firſt is, That my Client promotes
an Entertainment call'd a Maſquerade,
which in Fact, is nothing but a human
Catterwauling; but to ſhew how wide
the Spite of this flies from the Mark it
was level'd at, I ſhall anſwer, That my

Client

Client is utterly unable to bear any
Part in an Entertainment of that Nature.

The second is, That he keeps half a
dozen Miftreffes, and is unable (as I
faid above) to ufe any one of them ; fo
that you fee in this Reflection they come
into my own Opinion of him : But I
would afk then, where lies his Crime?
Is there not rather a negative Virtue
afcrib'd to him, in that he keeps fo many lew'd Women from purfuing their
own vicious Inclinations ?

The third Reflection is fo very fhock-
ing, that was I not refolv'd to go tho-
rough-ftitch in this Apology, I would
not have mention'd it, left this Tract of
mine fhould fall into the Hand of fome
Lady big with Child , and that is, That
my Client is as ugly as the Devil, or
the Knight of the ugly Face, and fuch
like : But in Anfwer to it, I fhall al-
ledge, That he did not make his Face
himfelf; and that by thefe Mafks he has
pafs'd Mufter amongft the Handfomeft,
and has had the Pleafure of feeing fome
of our firft rate Toafts in Difguifes (if
poffible) ugler than himfelf.

The fourth Reflection is, That he has
debauch'd the People ; but to this I anfwer, That he found them already debauch'd

bauch'd to his Hand, or he could ne'er
have succeeded as he has done.

The fifth Reflection is, That he designs
by these Entertainments of his, to introduce Popery, and the Pretender ; but
in Answer to this, I shall plead, That my
Client has necessarily taken the Oaths to
the Government, and abjur'd the Pretender, which the Lawyers tell us, is
all the Security required for any Man's
Fidelity ; and one Thing, I am sure of,
that no Change that can possibly happen, can be of more Advantage to him,
than what he enjoys at present : But as
'tis needless to rake further into the
Dirt, I shall only present my Readers
with the Report from the Committee of
Matrons appointed by my Client, to
state and examine the real Advantages,
arising from our present Masquerades.
The Countess of *Clingfast*, Chairwoman.

The REPORT.

IT having been made to appear to this
Committee, as well on the Oaths of
several hundreds of living Witnesses,
as by written Certificates, That there
has been within these eight Years last
past, above eight hundred Females cur'd
of that ill-favour'd Distemper, call'd the
Green-Sickness, by the frequent Use of
Masquerades,

Mafquerades, after all other Means were found ineffectual, not excepting the Steel Pills fold in *Duke's Place.*

Refolv'd then, That it is the Opinion of this Committee, that a Mafquerade rightly us'd, is a Specifick for that Diftemper.

It having likewife been made appear to this Committee, that more than 600 Women afflicted with Obftructions, Bearings-down, *&c.* have, at thefe Entertainments, found a pleafing, fafe, and effectual Cure.

Refolv'd likewife, That 'tis the Opinion of this Committee, that Mafquerades are extreamly helpful in fuch Cafes.

It having been further made appear alfo to this Committee, that 137 marry'd Ladies, fuppofed to have been Barren, have, by the frequent Ufe of thefe Entertainments, been made Fruitful.

Refolv'd likewife, That 'tis the Opinion of this Committee, that Mafquerades are a Specifick for Barrennefs, if curable.

It having been made appear alfo to this Committee, that near four hundred Females doom'd to the Arms of old, or otherwife,

otherwife, impotent Hufbands, have from the frequent Ufe of thefe Entertainments, receiv'd in good Part, Relief and Supply.

Refolv'd, That 'tis the Opinion of this Committee, that Impotency on the Man's Part, the coldeft, heavieft Curfe a Woman can labour under, is. in good Meafure fupply'd by Mafquerades.

It having been made appear likewife to this Committee, that fourfcore and fifteen Gentlewomen too ftrait lac'd, or aukard, to entertain their Hufbands, have from the frequent Ufe of Mafquerades, been made more capable of their Duty.

Refolv'd then, That 'tis the Opinion of this Committee, that thefe Entertainments have a very great Tendency, to make Ladies capable of pleafing their Hufbands.

It having likewife been made appear to this Committee, that an unfpeakable Number of well-bred Ladies (reftrain'd by their Characters from many convenient Liberties, enjoy'd by thofe in a lower Clafs) have been fadly opprefs'd with Spleen and Vapours, 'till by frequenting thefe Marfquerades, where they

they could aſſume the Liberty of talking, what pleas'd them beſt, without
bluſhing, they have found Amendment
of Health.

Reſolv'd then, That 'tis the Opinion
of this Committee, that Ladies ſhall
have Liberty to wear Maſks, at all ſuch
Times as they have Occaſion to twattle
of Humours, as are neceſſary to Health,
without the Expence of Bluſhes.

It having been farther made appear
too, to this Committee, that ſeveral Gentlemen are forc'd to check their natural Deſire of talking, unleſs at Maſquerades, becauſe conſcious of Underſtan-
dings inferiour to their Eſtates and
Honours.

Reſolv'd then, That 'tis the Opinion
of this Committee, that Maſks are ab-
ſolutely neceſſary to ſuch Gentlemen ;
and that therefore, they ſhould be allow'd to wear them in all Places, and at
all Times, in common with their Swords,
that they may talk their own Things
over in their own Way, without Reproach to their Quality.

This Committee having further taken
it into Conſideration, that Separations
of Man and Wife, which prov'd from
a mutual

a mutual Diflike of each other, and
Divorces occafion'd by the good Woman's being prov'd tardy, are fufficiently provided againft in Mafquerades; becaufe, if any Man diflikes his own Wife,
he may there have the Ufe of almoft
any other Man's, he finds prefent ; and
likewife, the Wife to, may be furnifh'd
with an agreeable Variety ; and if fome
Ladies are to frail too keep their Matters
to themfelves, they may there find a
fufficient Concealment.

So that this right reputable Committee is of Opinion, that Mafquerades fhall
be farther extended, in Order to extend
their great Ufefulnefs, that is, that in the
good Cities of *London* and *Weftminfter*,
there be two every Week, and one likewife weekly in every City and County
Town in *England* at leaft, Lent except-
ed, when 'tis (if ever) convenient to
abftain from all Kinds of Flefh; and that
for the Sake of Regularity, they be all
under the Licence and Direction of
Mr. *H———r.*

    C. *Clingfaft*, Chairwoman.

This Report was fent me by my Client, to lay before the Publick, and is
here fubmitted to the publick Opinion ;
he being refolv'd as far as is confiftent

E   with

with his Intereſt, to walk blamelefs for the Future. Thus having finiſh'd my Taſk, and receiv'd the Pay promis'd me by my Client, I ſhall lay down my Pen in full Aſſurance of never being oblig'd to take it up again in this Cauſe, or rather to hang it up in the Theatre in the *Hay-Market* as a Trophy, having gain'd a compleat Victory, and ſhall now prepare my ſelf with clean Linnen and ſtrong Jellies, to wait the Favours promis'd me by the Ladies.

F I N I S.

THE
CONDUCT
OF THE
STAGE
CONSIDER'D.

BEING

A Short Hiſtorical Account of its Original, Progreſs, various Aſpects, and Treatment in the
Pagan, Jewiſh and Chriſtian World.

Together with the Arguments urg'd againſt it, by
Learned Heathens, and by Chriſtians, both Antient
and Modern.

With Short REMARKS upon the Original and Pernicious
Conſequences of MASQUERADES.

---

*Humbly recommended to the Conſideration of thoſe who
frequent the* PLAY-HOUSES.

One Play-Houſe ruins more Souls than fifty Churches are able to ſave.
Bulſtrode's Charge to the Grand Jury of *Middleſex,* April the
21ſt, 1718.

LONDON;

Printed for Eman. Matthews, at the *Bible* in *Pater-
noſter-Row.* M, DCC XXI.
(Price Six Pence.)

The Conduct of the STAGE *consider'd.*

HE enfuing Treatife does not only account for the Original, Progrefs, Conduct, and Treatment of the Stage in the feveral Ages of the World, but alfo does, *en paſſant*, fhow, that as it is now ufually manag'd, it ought not to be permitted among Chriftians ; being generally calculated for the Meridian of Vice, and to give a Relifh to the frothy Pleafures of the vain part of Mankind, as Mr. *Collier* has abundantly prov'd. To give the greater Force to this Charge of Impiety againft the Stage, I fhall, in the moft concife and confpicuous manner, fhew, That,

I. THE Stage, with all its pompous Train, is of a Pagan Original, invented for the Honour and Worfhip of Dæmons.

II. EVEN Pagans, and among them fome who had not the greateft regard to Virtue, abominated Play-houfes as fo many Seminaries of Vice.

III. THE Primitive Church look'd upon the Stage as the Scene not only of Folly, but Impiety ; therefore the Chriftians, in thofe days, durft not frequent the publick Shews that were exhibited for the Entertainment of the People.

IV. THE Diverfions of the Stage have been difcountenanc'd by the wifeft States and Kingdoms, and even by thofe who, upon their firft Appearance, were fond of them, as the *Greeks* and *Romans.*

A   V. STAGE

V. Stage-Plays are no where authorized or allowed by the Church of *England* as such ; but every where condemn'd by the Purity of her Doctrine, and by some of her most eminent Lights.

VI. Among the Papists, who have almost converted all Religion into Plays, are found Enemies to the Stage.

VII. Conclude the whole, with proper Reflections.

Whoever will be at the pains of examining the several Discoveries made under these Heads, will soon see how the Corruption of the Stage has been a publick Nusance in all Ages, both among Pagans and Christians, Antient and Modern.

I

The Stage, with all its pompous Train, is of a Pagan Original, invented for the Honour and Worship of Demons.

Among the *Romans* there were several kinds of Games and Plays sacred to their Idols.

The first I shall mention were those they called the *Circensian, Floral, Cereal, Apollinar,* and *Capitoline.* These Plays were a part of their Devotion : An Actor was a kind of a Priest, the Theatre a Temple, and to frequent the Stage was a sort of Worship paid to the Devil in their Demons, according to the Fathers, who look'd upon the Play-house as the Temple of Satan, *Ecclesia Diaboli. Tertul. de Spectris, cb.*1C.

Valerius Maximus tells us of one *Valesius,* a rich *Roman,* being ill of the Plague, was, by the Direction of an evil Spirit, cured of it, by washing in hot Water taken from the Altar of *Proserpina ;* in recompence for which, the Spirit order'd his Patients to institute certain Plays to him. *Val. Max. lib.* 2. *cap.* 4.

Dionysius Halicarnasseus tells us, how in a time of great Mortality the Devil appear'd to one *T. Latinus,* in the shape of *Jupiter Capitolinus,* commanding him to tell the Citizens, That their Neglect of the Plays was the reason of that Judgment ; upon which they renew'd the Plays with greater Pomp, and the Plague ceased. *Latine, Dic Civibus mihi ludis Præsultatorem displicuisse, qui nisi magnifice instaurentur periculum Urbi fore. Antiq. Rom. lib.* vii. *p.*557. *Lugd.* 1561.

The Stage indeed may still pass for a Temple, since 'tis often more crowded than the Church, and its Performances too often entertain'd with greater Gust than those of the Pulpit. If a timely Check be not given to the wild Excursions of it, it will, I am afraid, in time reduce us to a necessity of

building

building Theatres faster than Churches, as they are already more magnificent than those sacred Edifices.

THE next *Roman* Diversions that I shall take notice of, is that which took in the common Stage-Players, by way of *Comedy* and *Tragedy*: These Scenick Diversions were Strangers at *Rome*, while the *Roman* Virtue retain'd its pristine Vigour, and were not seen there till three hundred eighty nine years after its Building, when appear'd certain Morris-Dancers, or Buffoons, who, by their frightful Figures, Gesticulations, and other Anticks, pretended to divert the People, that is, make them stare and laugh. I will begin,

1. WITH *Tragedy* (a Dramatick Performance upon the Theatre, wherein the Actions of Heroes are represented) which, in the beginning, was only a devotional Hymn sung by the Pagans in Honour of *Bacchus*, the God of Wine, who was ador'd by most Nations (except the *Scythians*, who thought it ridiculous to worship for a God one that made People Fools or mad.) The first Occasion was thus:

ICARIUS, who reign'd in *Attica*, about *A. M.* 2700. having taken a He-Goat, that had ravag'd his Vineyard, sacrific'd it to *Bacchus*: during that Ceremony, the People danc'd about the Altar, singing the Praises of that God; which Practice was annually observ'd, and call'd *Trigody*, a Vintage-Song, and afterwards *Tragody*, which we pronounce *Tragedy*, from Τεγγϑ, a Goat, and ῞Ωδη, a Song; so that Tragedy is as much as to say a Goat-Song.

THE Play-house still smells rank of that wanton Animal, according to *Salvian's* Doctrine, who says, In the Representations of Fornication, all the whole Body of the People are mental Fornicators; and they who, it may be, came clean to the Play, return Adulterers from the Theatres: *Omnis omnino Plebs fornicatur—adulteri revertuntur. De Gubern. Dei, Oxon.* 1635. *pag.* 191.

ALL pompous Diversions are dangerous to a Christian Life, but none more so than these Plays; for they give so nice and natural a Representation of the Passions, that they soon affect the Heart, especially with that of dishonourable Love, when represented as chaste and innocent; for the more innocent it appears, the more easily it insinuates itself. Hence it is, too many go from a Play, so charm'd with the Pleasures of Love, that they are prepar'd to put in practise what Immodesties they saw represented there. For as *Minutius Felix* expresses it, 'Sometimes a luscious Actor shall
' whine you into Love, and give the Disease he counterfeits.'

HORACE

HORACE afcribes the Invention of Tragedy to *Thefpis*; who brought forth his Satyrs in an open Cart from which the Actors rehears'd their Poems, their Faces being daub'd with Dregs of Wine ; or, according to *Suidas*, painted with Cerufe and Vermilion, in imitation of the Satyrs, who are reprefented with a ruddy Vifage.

Ignotum Tragicæ Genus inveniffe Camænæ,
Dicitur & Plauftris vexiffe Poemata Thefpis. **Hor.**

BUT the Refinement of the Stage is attributed to *Æfchy-lus*, who introduc'd Vizards, fettled two Actors for the Epi-fodes, invented Habits fuiting the Perfons they reprefented, as alfo the *Cothurni* ; Buskins to heighten their Stature, that they might appear like Heroes.

SOPHOCLES, a *Greek* Tragedian, added much towards the Perfection of Tragedy, painted the Scene with Decorations, according to the nature of the Subjects that were to be reprefented.

2. I proceed to *Comedy*, which is a Play-houfe Performance, wherein the common Accidents of human Life are reprefented.

THESE Comick Plays alfo at firft, were nothing but a kind of Hymn the Pagans fung to *Bacchus*, dancing about the Altar, on which they facrific'd a He-Goat to him. *Athenæus.*

IT receiv'd the name of Comedy, when the *Athenians* made ufe of this Ceremony in their City ; and added the Chorus of Mufick, with Set and Figure-Dances. Then this was called Tragedy, and the Ceremony; as practifed in the Country, retain'd the name of Comedy, or Village-Song ; from the *Greek* word Κωμη, a Village, and Ωδη, a Song or Hymn, of which the Popifh Wake-Songs are Imitations.

PLATO tells us, That the Commemoration of their De-mons was celebrated with Hymns. Thus the *Greeks*, who are fuppofed to be the firft Inventors of them, had their fo-lemn Hymns, called κληϊκυς ὑμνῳ, which they fung to their propitious Demons.

THE *Romans* alfo had their *Affamenta*, or peculiar Hymns, fung to the fame particular Deity ; as their *Janualia, Juno-nia, Minervalia* : the Songs, which the Papifts fing to their canonized Saints on their Holy-Days, are Copies of thefe Pa-gan Hymns, that were only rude Effays towards Dramatick Poetry.

THAT the Pagan Plays were part of thofe Solemnities they perform'd to their Demons, which indeed were Devils,

is

is evident from St. *Auftin*, who fhews out of *Varro*, that
Plays were not wont to be celebrated to any but the Gods.
De Civit. Dei, lib. viii. *cap.* 26. Thus we fee that the Diverfions of the Stage are of a Pagan Extraction, and were part
of the Pagan Devotions.

CHRISTIAN Virtue muft needs run very low, when fuch
Diverfions are acted in contempt of the true God, and to ridicule facred things, as were inftituted by Heathens in Honour of their fictitious Deities. Here I muft alfo obferve, that
the Bible forbids us to imitate the Cuftoms and Ufages of the
Heathens: Jer. 10. 3. *Thus faith the Lord, learn not the way of
the Heathen, for the Cuftoms of the People are vain.* Nay more;
the very mentioning of Heathen Gods (unlefs it be by way
of Abhorrence) is forbidden: Exod. 23. 13. *Make no mention
of the Names of other Gods, neither let it be heard out of thy
Mouth.*

Now therefore by going to the Playhoufe, and there,
with Approbation, hearing the Names of other Gods echoing
round the Theatre, 'Thou defieft the Precepts and Prohibi-
'tions of thy God ; thou art an Enemy to Chriftianity, in
'that thou dareft to encourage thofe Plays, that are not only
'fome of the vain Cuftoms of the Heathens, but Monu-
'ments of their Idolatry, as they were Sacrifices to the De-
'vil.'

THE Obfervation of Pagan Cuftoms is not only condemn'd
by Scripture, but by the Primitive Church.

THE Synod of *Trullus*, held at *Conftantinople, A. D.* 683.
orders all thofe to be excommunicated, who did not renounce Heathen Cuftoms and Practices. *Ethnica Inftitut. Caranz. Can. 51.*

BY Canon 71. thofe who ftudy'd the Civil Law, were not
to ufe Heathenifh Cuftoms, nor go to the Theatre, nor wear
the Scenical Habit of the Stage. *Græcis moribus uti non opor-
tere. Caranza.*

TERTULLIAN condemn'd the wearing a Laurel-Crown by
a Chriftian Soldier in his Triumph, becaufe it was of an
idolatrous (and infernal) Original, and worn by the Vaffals
of Hell. *De Coron. Mil Can.* vii.

THE Council of *Africa* forbids Chriftians to make Feafts
and Sports upon Birth-Days, becaufe they had their Original
from the *Gentiles. Can.* 63. *in the* Gr.

THE Fathers thought it finful to obferve any Relicks of
Paganifm, and accordingly renounced them ; as their *Sports,
Recreations, Morris-Dances, Mummings, Lotteries, New-Years
Gifts*

Gifts, Dancings, Feſtivals, &c. Theſe, they ſaid, · were invented by the Devil, it being part of the Worſhip he requir'd of them? they were conſecrated to his Honour, and appropriated to his Service by his ſpecial Direction: and therefore one of the Biſhops of the Church calls the Playhouſe the *Devil's Church,* and *Plays* his *Pomps. Tertul. de Spectac.*

THESE Plays, in their firſt Deſign, were to pacify the Anger of the Gods; as *Jupiter, Bacchus, Neptune, Flora, Muſes, Apollo, Diana, Venus,* or ſome other Dunghil-Idol which the Pagans ador'd ; to whoſe Honour, Names, and Memories they were celebrated, as appears from *Plutarch, Dion. Halicarn. Val. Maximus, Livy,* as well as from the concurrent Teſtimonies of the Fathers.

How ſad is it to ſee the Chriſtian Stage crowded with Pagan Gods (whoſe Names ſhould not be ſo much as mention'd without juſt Indignation) and the Supreme Being often revil'd, through the ill Language that is ſometimes given to theſe Heathen Numens.

HENCE that warm Exclamation of *Clemens Alexandrinus* againſt the *Gentiles: Oh Impiety ! you have made the Theatre Heaven, you have made God himſelf an Act ; that which is holy, you have derided in the Perſons of Devils,* ᾿Οἴμοι τῆς ἀϑεόϊηΙϚ *Opera Colon.* 1688. *adm. ad Gentes, pag.* 39.

THE Third Council of *Carthage* forbids Chriſtians to attend the Stage, becauſe the Actors are Blaſphemers. *Cap.* 2. *ſecund. Caranz. See Salv. & Chryſoſtom.*

THO God forbids us to invoke Idols, or ſwear by them, yet what more common in Plays than, in contempt of the ſacred Oracles, to implore the Aid of *Jove, Juno, Apollo, Bacchus, Minerva*——than to ſwear by *Jove!* by *Mars!* by *Venus* ——and to exclaim, *Oh Jove ! Oh Muſes! Oh Cupid! Oh Venus! Oh ye Powers! Oh ye Gods!* Now all theſe are infernal Deities, and the Practice of our Actors herein is a direct Imitation of the Heathens, who ſupplicated their departed Heroes as Gods, in a fabulous ſporting manner, eſpecially in their Poems and Interludes. *Athanaſ. contr. Gent. Lugd.* 1532.

THE Sixth Council of *Conſtantinople* inflicts the Penalty of Excommunication upon thoſe who ſwear by the Heathen Gods. *Jurantes Juramenta Ethnica*——*Caranz. Can.* 94. 81 *of St.* Baſil.

CAN any thing be more unbecoming the Character of a Chriſtian, than to act and applaud theſe idolatrous Imprecations, and make a Jeſt of that, which, in reality, is a Profanation of the Eternal Name ?   II.

II.

EVEN *Pagans, and among them some who had not the greatest Regard to Virtue, abominated Play-Houses as so many Seminaries of Vice.*

THESE *Shews* were invented, 'tis true, by some of themselves, receiv'd and entertain'd with Applause, but could not obtain the universal Vogue ; the gross Obscenities with which their Devotional Games and Plays were generally intermix'd, render'd them odious to the thinking part of Mankind, even in those dark Ages.

THUS their *Floralia* were made with all dissolute Sports, their Women dancing naked ; yet the abandon'd Heathens were not so immers'd in Luxury and Darkness, but among them were found those who abhorr'd these Representations of the Stage, because injurious to Good-Manners, and the common Rights of Virtue. I'll begin,

1. WITH *Plato*, chief of the Academicks, about the 325th Year of *Rome*, who would suffer no Stage-Plays in his Commonwealth, because those Diversions were dangerous to Morality, and consequently to Government. *De Rep. Dial.*

2. ARISTOTLE, chief of the Peripateticks, born about 384 years before Christ, forbids the seeing of *Comedies* to young People, because it would poison their Minds ; and advises all Princes to banish Smut out of their Kingdoms.

3. XENOPHON, who dy'd in the CVth Olympiad, commends the *Persians* for not suffering their Youth to hear Comedies. Sir *John Chardin*, in his Travels into *Persia*, tells us, they still take very great care in educating their Youth, and don't generally suffer them to mix with the Crowd till they are of Age ; so that when they come abroad, they appear with an Air of Modesty and Gravity. *2d and 3d Vol.*

4. TULLY, born the 648th of *Rome*, declaims against Plays and licentious Poems as the Plague of Society ; and in particular against *Comedies, that subsisted only by Lewdness:* Manners must be mightily reform'd by these Actors, who make Love and Lewdness a Deity ; therefore advises the *Romans* to abandon them, left they should be corrupted by them, as the *Grecians* were, to their Ruin. *Tuscul. Quest. l.iv.*

HE blames *Trabea* and *Cæcilius*, two Comick Poets, for magnifying Love-Adventures, making *Cupid* a God, and flourishing too much upon the Satisfactions of Sense ; he complains also of *Tragedy*, how, in many Instances, it baffled the Force of Virtue.

B 5. LIVY

5. LIVY, the Hiſtorian, who dy'd in the 4th Year of *Ti-beſius*, ſays, That Plays were brought in upon the ſcore of Religion, to appeaſe the Gods in time of a Plague ; but the Remedy prov'd worſe than the Diſeaſe, and the Atonement more infectious than the Plague ; for the Plays did more hurt to the Mind, than the Peſtilence to the Body. *Hiſt.* Tom. 1. *l:b.* vi, vii. *Cantabrigiæ* 1679.

6. VALERIUS MAXIMUS, who liv'd in the days of *Tibe-rius*, having deſcrib'd the Theatre in its Riſe, Progreſs, and Decorations, tells us how fatal the Performances of it were to Religion, and how the *Romans*, as they grew rich, added Pomp and Magnificence to the Plays, the Toleration of which he look'd upon as a Blemiſh to the *Roman* State.

7. SENECA, who dy'd in the 12th of *Nero*'s Reign, com-plains how the *Roman* Youth were generally corrupted by the Countenance which *Nero* gave to the Stage, and to all thoſe Acts that indulg'd the ſenſitive Part. In Stage-Plays, adds he, Vice gets an eaſy Paſſage into the Heart, the Play-houſe is the high Road to the Brothel-houſe ; therefore ad-viſes *Lucilius* to avoid all Plays, and laments the frequent Concourſe of the *Roman* Youth to them. *Seneca, Ep.* 7. *nil tam damnoſun.*——

8. SOCRATES, pronounc'd by the Oracle the wiſeſt of Men, look'd upon Plays not only as lying unprofitable Diver-ſions, but unbecoming, and pernicious Paſtimes ; which caus'd *Ariſtophanes*, a *Greek* Comedian, to traduce him upon the Stage. His Invectives againſt him appear in his *Comedy of the Clouds. Vid. Vitam.*

9. TACITUS tells us how the *Greeks* and *Latins* exercis'd the Art of a Stage-Player after a very immodeſt manner—— that *C. Pompeius* was blam'd by the anti-nt Men for building a permanent Theater ; for in times paſt Plays were ſet forth upon moveable Scaffolds, and the People beheld them ſtand-ing, and were not allow'd Seats, leſt they ſhould ſpend too much time at thoſe idle Diverſions. *Ovid* ſays, that in his time they ſat upon Seats made of Turf :

In gradibus ſedit Populus de ceſpite faɕis.

THE Hiſtorian complains how the *Roman* Virtue and Diſ-cipline had been corrupted by the Stage ; and how whole Days and Nights were taken up by thoſe Plays, and no time left to be honeſt. *Annal. Amſterod.* 1678. *lib.* 14. *cap.* 20. *l.* 13. *c.* 6, 7.

IN

IN his 4th Book he informs us how the *Ofcian Play*, that was so pleasing to the People, grew to such Insolence, that 'twas suppress'd by the Senate, and the Actors banish'd. *Lib. 4. cap. 14.*

HE inveighs much against *Nero*, for introducing all kinds of Vice by *Stage-Plays*.

10. PLUTARCH, in his Morals, does not only condemn Plays as lascivious Vanities, and contagious Evils; but *Poetry* itself as full of Lyes, and quotes *Socrates* as a Voucher.

AMONG all holy and consecrated things, says *Cowley*, which the Devil has alienated from the Service of the Deity, as Altars, Temples——there is none he so universally and so long usurp'd as Poetry. *His Preface, towards the end of it.*

11. OVID, that wanton Poet, informs *Augustus*, that Playhouses are the Nurseries of all Wickedness, the Congress of Adulteries, and therefore advises him to demolish them.

> *Ut tamen hoc fateor, ludi quoque femina præbent*
> ——*Nequitiæ: tolli tota Theatra jube.*
> *Peccandi Caufam quam multis fæpe dederunt*
> ——*Tollatur Circus.*   De Triftib. I. 2.

IN his Poem, *de Arte Amandi*, he tells his leacherous Affociates, That the Play-houses were the best Fairs for unchaste Bargains, the most commodious Haunts for amorous Fellows, and only Places for Panders and Whores.

> *Sed tu præcipue curvis venare Theatris*
> *Hæc loca funt votis fertiliora tuis,*
> *Illic invenies quid ames*——
> *Notat fibi quifquam Puellam.*   lib. 1.

Then adds, 'Twas impossible for Parents, or Husbands, to keep their Children and Wives chaste, while so many Playhouses were suffer'd in the City. *De Art. Amand. l. 3.*

> *Quid faciet cuftos cum fint tot in Urbe Theatra?*

IN another Place advises all those who would live chastely, to withdraw from the Play-house, and to throw away all Play-Books, amorous Poems, especially *Tibullus* and *Callimachus*, yea and his own wanton Verses:

At

At tanti tibi fit non indulgere Theatris
——Teneros ne tangas Poetas——Callimachum fugito——
Carmina quis potuit tuto legiſſe Tibulli.

De Remed. Am. lib. 2.

12. PROPERTIUS, an obſcene Poet, cries out againſt the Theatres as the Inſtruments of his Ruin. *Ob nimis Exitio na-ta Theatra meo.. Eleg. Amʃt. ad Demipb.* xviii. *p.* 158.

13. ISOCRATES, a *Greek* Orator, exclaims againſt all Actors and Players, as ſcurrilous, and miſchievous, and intolerable Plagues to a City. *Orat. ad Nic. & Orat. de Pace.*

14. C. PLINIUS SECUNDUS, in his Panegyrick to the Emperor *Trajan,* ſtiles Stage-Plays effeminate Arts, altogether unbecoming Men, and applauds the Emperor for baniſhing them out of the *Roman* Empire, whoſe Honour they had ſully'd, and whoſe Virtue they had corrupted; therefore calls them *intolerable Miſchiefs. Paneg. Trajan. Diſt. Coloniæ Allob, pag.* 38.

15. SOLON, one of the wiſe Men of *Greece,* condemn'd Plays as Evils not to be ſuffer'd in a City. *Plutarc. in, vit. Theſpim Tragædias agere & docere probibui:——Diogen. in vit. p.* 46. *Lugd.* 1592.

16. AMMIANUS MARCELLLINUS, the Hiſtorian, ſpeaks againſt Stage-Plays as the great Corruptions of the *Roman* State. *Hiſt. l.* 28. *c.* 10.

17. I AM, ſays M. *Antoninus,* to thank my Great Grand-father for not running the risk of a publick Education, and for providing me Maſters at home, from whom I have learnt not to overvalue the *Diverſions of the Theatre.*

MANY more Heathens might be produc'd, as *Quintilian, Macrobius, Juvenal, Horace, V. Paterculus, Diod. Siculus,* &c. but theſe are ſufficient to ſhew in what repute Virtue was among ſome of them, and how they abhorr'd the Stage as an Enemy to all Good. And ſhall the Followers of the mortify'd Jeſus countenance theſe Theatrical Entertainments, which Heathens cenſur'd as the Plague of Societies, and Ruin of common Morality?

THE Compoſitions of ſeveral of the old Dramatiſts, 'tis true, were full of amorous and wanton Intrigues, and the Froth of an exuberant Wit; and ſubſtract theſe out of moſt of the *Engliſh* Plays, and there will remain nothing but an empty Theatre, and a forſaken Hive. Kick off Vice from the Stage, and let nothing be repreſented there but Virtue

in

in all its Attractives, and there is an end of the Play-house.
Exit Actor.

III.

THE *Primitive Church look'd upon the Stage as the Scene not only of Folly, but Impiety ; therefore the Christians in those days
durst not frequent the publick Shews that were exhibited for the
Entertainment of the People.*

THIS is so notorious, that the Heathens objected it as a
Crime against the Christians to be absent from them ; as
appears from *Minutius Felix,* a famous *Roman* Lawyer, who
flourish'd about the Year of Christ 220. with whose Opinion
I begin.

1. THE *Romans,* says *Cæcilius* the Heathen in *Minutius,* go-
vern and enjoy the World, while you Christians are careful
and mopish, abstaining even from lawful Pleasures ; you vi ·
fit not Shews, nor are present at the Pomps : you abhor the
holy Games——a melancholy ghastly People ye are——

TRUE, says *Octavius,* we Christians refrain from the Play-
house, because of its intolerable Corruptions——We can't
be present at the Plays without great Sin and Shame. *Meritò
malis Voluptatibus——& Spectaculis abstinemus——Min. Felix,
Oxon.* 1662. *pag.* 41.

2. LACTANTIUS, who liv'd *A. D.* 303. speaking of Tragedies and Comedies, says, They only serve to excite Lust,
and the more artful the Actors are in their Representations,
the more Mischief they do——*Et Comicæ Fabulæ de stupris
Virginum loquuntur aut Amoribus Meretricum ; & quo magis sunt
eloquentes——Item Tragica Hist.——vitanda ergo spectacula om-
nia. Lib.* vi. *c.* 20. *Basil. Ed.* 1563. *p.* 371.

3. TERTULLIAN, who liv'd *A. C.* 192. having spent six
or seven Chapters in proving Plays to be unlawful, and in
dissuading the Christians from them, says, *The Devil help'd
them with Stilts ;* i. e. to make them look like Heroes of the
first Figure ; calls the Play-house the Sink of Debauchery,
the Chappel of *Venus,* or a Bawdy-house : *Consistorium Impudicitiæ——Tragœdos Cothurnis extulit——Sacrarium Veneris. cap.*
10. *&* 17.

So many Persons as fit in the Play-house, so many unclean
Spirits are present ; *tot illic. ibid.*

THIS Father gives an Account of a Christian Woman,
who, going to the Play-house, was there possess'd by the
Devil ; and when, at his casting out, was ask'd by the Ex-
orcists, How he durst enter into a Christian ? he answer'd, I
found

found her upon my Ground : *In meo eam inveni*——*De Spect:*
c. 26. Franak. 1597.

He tells us of Danger in the beft-complexion'd Entertainments of the Stage ; look therefore, adds he, upon all the engaging and pleafing Sentences, as Honey dropping from the Bowels of a Toad, or the Bag of a Spider. *Ibid.*

4. Theophilus of *Antioch*, who flourifh'd about the Year 168. looks upon Plays as dangerous Sports, therefore forbids Men to frequent them, that their Eyes and Ears be not polluted : Ἀλλ᾽ ἐδὲ τὰς λοιπὰς θεωείας ὁρᾷν χρὴ ἵνα μὴ κολυμώ-
θας. *Ad Autol. lib.* 3. *pag.* 233. *Oxon.* 1684.

5. Cyprian, who dy'd 258. proves it to be altogether unlawful for Chriftians to attend the Diverfions of the Play-houfe, which he calls the *Devil's Scaffold*, where the Holy Scripture was blended with Theatrical Vanities, and profan'd. He adds, That thofe Chriftians, who attended the Stage, did not only approve the Folly and Madnefs of the Heathens, but renounc'd their Baptifm——That many Virgins, who frequented the Play-houfe, made fhipwreck of their Chaftity. *Diaboli Spectaculum. de Spec. p.* 460, 461. *Excudeb. Job. le Preux,* M.D.XC.III.

6. Clemens Alexandrinus, who liv'd *A. D.* 192. declares againft Stage-Plays as Schools of Impiety, peftilent Sports, and Introductions to all kinds of Immorality ; he calls the Theatre the *Chair of Peftilence* ; ἐδὲ ᾽Απεικόζως——τὰ διάζεα καθίδεαν λοιμῶν. *Lib.* iii. *p.* 254. *Colon.* 1688.

7. Chrysostom, who was born 354. with great Warmth reproves the People of *Antioch* for their reforting to Play-houfes, which he ftiles the *Devil's Conventicles* ; and fays, He would never ceafe Preaching till he had diffipated that *Devilifh Theatre*. Stage-Plays he calls the *Devil's Pomps*, *Fables of Satan, Demonical Myfteries, impure Food of the Devil* ; *nec ufquam prorfus quiefcam, quoad ufque Diabolicum illud difpergam Theatrum. Hom.* 7. *in Mat. Vid. Hom. in Eph. Colof. de David & Saul.*

Speaking of *David* and *Bathfheba*, he fays, *David* faw her, and was wounded in his Eye. Let thofe hear this who contemplate the Beauty of others, and who are poffefs'd with an unruly Defire after Stage-Plays, who fay, we behold them without hurt. What hear I ? *David* is hurt, and art not thou ? He is wounded, and can I truft to thy Strength ? Did he fall who had fo great a meafure of the Spirit ? And canft thou ftand ? Yet he beheld not an Harlot, but an honeft Woman, and that not in the Theatre, but at home ; but

thou

thou beholdeft an Harlot in the Play-houfe, where even the
very Place itfelf makes the Soul liable to Punifhment.

NEITHER doft thou only fee, but heareft unclean Words
and obfcene Songs ; thou art not Iron or Stone, but a Man
fubject to the common Frailty of Nature——We can't ferve
two Maſters ; now he who goes to Church one day, and to
Stage-Plays another day, ferves two Maſters. *Hom.* 1. *on
Pfal.* 50. *& Hom. in Pfal.* 119.

8. ST. AUSTIN, born *A. D.* 335. does not only look upon
Stage-Plays as improper Diverfions for Chriftian People, but
counts them more abominable than Sacrifices offer'd to Idols.
De Civit. Dei, l. iii. *ad Marcel. & lib.* 2. *c.* 28. *p.* 77. *Edit. in
Octavo, Vol.* 1. *Excud. Jac. Stoer,* M. D. XC. VI.

IN another Place he calls *Plays the Pomps of the Devil*,
which we renounce in Baptifm : What art thou, Oh Chriftian, fays he, when thou profeffeft one thing, and doeft another ? Going one while into the Church to pray, and a while
after into the Play-houfe to cry out impudently with Stage-
Players——*Poſt modicum in Spectaculis cum Hiſtrionibus impu-
dice clamare. De Symbol. ad Catech. l.* 4.

ST. AUSTIN, in his Confeffions, reflects with Grief and
Shame on his going to Play-houfes, when young, and on the
Detriment he receiv'd by it. *Lib.* 3. *c.* 1, 2. *l.* 4. *c.* 1, 2. *l.* 6.
c. 7, 8.

9. ISIDORE PELUSIOTA, who flourifh'd about the Year
412. fays of Stage-Players, That their great end is to draw
Men to Sin ; and if the Spectators were made better, the
Occupation of Players would go to wreck. *Ep. ad Hier.*

10. ATHENAGORAS, who flourifh'd, *A. D.* 177, in his
Apologeticks for the Chriftian Religion, fays, The Spectacles of
the Theatre, the Games, the Gladiators, you Heathens generally admire, we Chriftians think it finful to look on them,
and therefore abftain from all Sights of this kind. *Ad finem,*
Oxon. 1682.

11. CYRIL of *Jerufalem*, who liv'd 350. calls Plays the
Devil's Pomps, which we renounce in our Baptifm. *Catech. Myſt.*

12. GREGORY NAZIANZEN, who flourifh'd 370. fpeaking of Stage-Players, fays, They count nothing filthy or
bafe, but Modefly; that they are the Propagaters of all
Lewdnefs, and that the Playhoufe is the Wanton's Shop : *Ni-
hil turpe ducunt præter Modeſtiam.*

13. EPIPHANIUS fays, The Catholick and Apoſtolical
Church damns all Theatres and Stage-Plays, Ἀποκηρυσσει Θεα-
τες. *L.* 3. *Tom.* 2. *p.* 1107. *Ed. Par.* 1622   14. SAL-

14. SALVIAN, a Priest, or as some say Bishop of *Marseilles*, who writ in the Vth Century, under *Zeno* the Emperor, says, There is nothing either sinful or vain, which is not acted in the publick Shews——*Nil fermè vel Criminum vel Flagitiorum est quod in Spectaculis non sit. De Gubern. Dei. Oxon.* CIƆ.IƆC.XXXIII. *p.* 186. I shall only speak, *adds he,* of the Cirques and Theatres where such things are acted, that a Man can't so much as speak of, yea remember them, without defiling himself; *p.* 189.

HE calls Plays Deluders of our Hopes, Cheats of Life, and Repast of the Devil, *pag.* 193. for while we divert ourselves in the Theatre, we perish, according to the sacred Text : Prov. 10.23. *It is as Sport to a Fool to do Mischief.*

So, in like manner, while we are sporting among those filthy and disgraceful Sights, we commit Wickedness, and our Danger is the greater; because tho they seem to be outwardly innocent, yet they are most pernicious——for there the Salvation of Christian People is destroy'd, and the Majesty of God prophan'd by sacrilegious Superstitions; for *Minerva* is honour'd in the Places for Exercise, *Venus* in the Theatres, *Neptune* in the Cirques, *Mars* in the Amphitheatre, *Mercury* in the Wrestling-Places. In one place there is Immodesty, in another Lasciviousness, in another Madness, and the Devil in them all : nay, all the Devils in Hell are in every one of the Places of these Pastimes; for they preside over the Places dedicated to their Worship—*Alibi est Impudicitia, alibi Lascivic—ubique Dæmon—Præsident sedibus suo cultui dedicatis. p.* 210.

WHEN the *Bishops* of the *Church* met in Council, they took into Consideration the *Evils* of the *Stage,* and provided against them accordingly.

THE Council of *Laodicea* (present most of the Bishops of *Asia*) held about the Year 364. forbids Clergymen to be present at Plays and Theatrical Shews, that were then us'd at Weddings or other Feasts, and orders them to get out of the House before the Maskers and Actors enter'd——*Antequam Thymelici ingrediantur surgere eos & abire. Caranz.Can.*54.

THIS *Laodicean* Council is confirm'd by the *Trullan* Council held in *Constantinople, A. D.* 683. By *Can.* 71. those who study the Civil Law are forbid to go into the Theatre, or use Heathenish Customs.

BY the third Council of *Carthage, A. D.* 401. no Laymen, or Clergymens Sons, are to be Actors or Spectators of publick Shews (*Caranz. Can.* 11.) because 'tis unworthy of Christians

ftians to be prefent in a Place where Blafphemies are fpo-
ken. By Can. 35. Actors of Plays, and fuch like Apoftates,
fhall not be deny'd the Communion, upon their Repen-
tance.

THE fourth Council of Carthage, about A. D. 401. prefent
two hundred and fourteen Bifhops; commands young Con-
verts to abftain from Stage-Plays, and excommunicates thofe
that refort to 'em, and not to Church, on folemn Days. Can.
86. & 88. Surius, Tom. 1:

THE firft Council of Arles, held about the Year 397. or
399. ordains, That thofe Chriftians who acted upon the Theatre, fhould be excommunicated while they follow'd thofe
Employments. Can. 4. & 5. This Decree is renew'd by the
fecond Council at Orleans.

BY the African Code it appears, that Stage-Players were
rank'd among Apoftates. Can. 45: Gr: 49.

THE Women Actors were counted fo fcandalous; that
whoever marry'd any of 'em, made himfelf uncapable of
being a Clergyman by the Apoftolical Canons. Caranza
Can. 18. ——in Uxorem duxit——aliquam——

THE Eliberine Council decrees, That if Chriftian Women,
or their Husbands, lend their Garments for the Shews, they
fhall be excommunicated for three Years. Caranz. Can. 57;
And by Can. 62. 'tis declared, That an Actor of Plays, or a
Comedian, who would turn Chriftian, fhould not be receiv'd
till he renounc'd his Theatrical Profeffion, and to be excommunicated if ever he return'd to it.

THE fixth Council of Conftantinople, held about the Year
680. which confifted almoft of Bifhops, obliges all Chriftians to renounce thofe Plays and Interludes, and excommunicates thofe who oppugn this Canon. Surius, Tom. 4.
Caranza, Can. 51.

SYNODUS Francica under Pope Zachary, about the Year
742. decrees, That the People of God make no Pagan Interludes, but renounce and abominate all the Uncleanneffes
of Gentilifm. Surius.

THE fecond Nicene Council, held about 785. according
to Baronius, where there were prefent three or four hundred
Bifhops, condemns Stage-Plays, and all Theatrical Sports.

SYNODUS Turconenfis under Charles the Great, about the
Year 813. determines that all Chriftians fhould avoid Stage-
Plays.

CONCILIUM Parifienfe under Lewis and Lotharius, about
the Year 829. fays; It better becomes holy Men to mourn
G   than

than to laugh at the Scurrilities, foolish Speeches, and obscene Jests of Stage-Players.———*Sanctis Viris*———*quibus magis convenit lugere. Can.* 58.

THE *Lateran Council, A. D.* 1215. consisting of two Patriarchs, seventy Archbishops, four hundred Bishops, eight hundred Abbots and Priors, condemns Tumblers, Jesters, and Stage-Players.

SYNODUS *Lingonensis,* about 1404. forbids Plays, especially the *Charcovian,* in which they used Vizards in the Shape of Devils, (a Play in nature of a Mask) under pain of Excommunication, and Forfeiture of 10 *l.*

CONCILIUM *Coloniense,* about 1549. complains how Monasteries were infected with Comedies and Stage-Plays, and provides against that Infection.

CONCILIUM *Mediolanense,* 1560. absolutely forbids Morris-Dances at all Times, and all other Plays on solemn Days. *Cap. de Fest. Lib. Tom.* 4. In the Chapter *de Histrionib.* they admonish Princes and Magistrates to banish out of their Territories all Stage-Players, Tumblers, Jugglers, Jesters, and all Reprobates of this kind.

I SHALL conclude this Article with the National Protestant Synod at *Rockel, A. D.* 1571. which says, ' It shall not ' be lawful for any Christians to act, or be present at any ' Comedies, Tragedies, Plays, Interludes, or any other such ' Sports———considering that they have always been oppos'd, ' condemn'd, and suppress'd in and by the Church, as bring- ' ing along with them the Corruption of good Manners.'

FROM these Quotations it appears, that the Profession of Stage-Players has been always counted unlawful and scandalous by the Christian Church ; and that Magistrates and Ministers did in their several Capacities contribute their Endeavours towards the Suppression of the Play-Houses.

THE Bishops of the Church did in all Ages condemn the Stage, looking upon the Entertainments of it as both shameful and dangerous, and therefore excommunicated the Players, as the Blemish of the Church. Nor did they censure these Diversions only because of idolatrous Mixtures, but because of their malevolent Influence upon Religion, as Mr. *Collier* has proved in his second Defence.

THERE are none among those who are acquainted with Ecclesiastical History, but know how the Primitive Christians thought themselves obliged not only to avoid criminal Pleasures, such as Debauchery, and those that were (at least) dangerous, as the Comedies and Publick Shews, but

also

alſo all unprofitable Pleaſures, that had no other end but the meer Entertainment of the Senſes; yea, would rather die than call *Jupiter a God*, as he is ſtiled in Stage-Plays. *Ad mortem uſque contendere Chriſtianos ne Jovem Deum appellent : Origen contr. Celſum, Tom. 4. l. 1. let. 1. printed 1512.*

BUT you'll ſay our Stage is reform'd :

BY no means, but rather grown worſe, as having found out the *Italian* Secret of Poiſoning Mankind; therefore the Primitive Arguments againſt them remain in their full Force.

Now, have the Fathers of the Chriſtian Church always declared againſt Plays as Publick Nurſeries of Profaneneſs, and ſhall the Sons and Daughters of the Church of *England* countenance and ſupport thoſe lewd Aſſociations? And did the Biſhops of the Church in its corrupt State alſo paſs ſo many ſevere Cenſures upon the Theatre, and ſhall the Children of the Reformation vindicate it? Shall thoſe who are Members of the true Apoſtolick Church, ſtain their Chriſtian Character, by reſorting to thoſe Places, where evil Communications corrupt good Manners? Shall thoſe who attend the Prayers of the Church, who eat and drink at the Sacred Altar, defile themſelves with the Abominations of the Heathens? Shall we encourage thoſe ludicrous Diverſions, that have been the Averſion not only of the beſt Chriſtians in all Ages, but of ſober Heathens? To put up the Stage therefore, is to pull down the Church.

WERE the Primitive Clergy now alive, would they have encouraged the Licentiouſneſs of the modern Stage, or allow'd thoſe Sallies of profane Wit, that invite Man thither? Would not they have play'd the Artillery of the Church againſt thoſe Forts of Darkneſs? Doubtleſs the Satire of the Pulpit would at leaſt have thunder'd as loud as the Blaſphemies of the Stage.

WHERE are the Succeſſors of thoſe Holy Fathers of the Church? Oh ye Miniſters of the Altar awake! rouſe up yourſelves, and ſound the Alarm in the Holy Mount. For never was the Church more in Danger from the Stage, (that *Chair of Peſtilence,* as *Cl. Alexandrinus* calls it; that Dramatick Bawdy houſe, as *Tertullian* calls *Pompey's Theatre.*) The vaſt Crowds of *Italians* that are lately come over, and now roam about the great City, will pull down faſter than you can build up, if you, Gentlemen of the Sacred Order, be not Co-operators with the Magiſtrate in ſapping the Foundations of the Stage.

WHAT Succefs can you hope for in the Pulpit, while thefe Abominations are indulged, while thefe unhallowed Groves and high Places of Immorality are frequented ? *Vid. Occafional Paper.*

SHALL Fathers, General Councils, and the whole Current of Antiquity, yea, uncultivated Heathens, damn the Corruptions of the Stage, and you fit ftill? How long will ye fuffer the Lambs of your Flock to be worry'd by thofe Wolves in Sheep's Cloathing? Why don't you thunder out the Anathema's of the Church againft the Theatre, from whence Virtue is banifh'd for its Serioufnefs, and where Lewdnefs is Factor for Hell?

IV.

THE *Diverfions of the Stage have been difcountenanced by the wifeft States and Kingdoms, and even by thofe who upon their firft Appearance were fond of them, as the* Greeks *and* Romans.

SOME Nations have fupprefs'd the Stage, and banifh'd the Actors out of their Countries, as the Primitive Chriftians threw them out of the Church. We'll begin,

1. WITH the *Athenians,* who were none of the worft Enemies to the Stage; thefe made a Law, that no Judge of the *Areopagus* [*Senate-Houfe*] fhould write a Comedy, looking upon it at leaft as an unreputable Part of Poetry, as well as an Indignity to his Office.

THEMISTOCLES, the famous *Athenian* General, made another Law, that no Magiftrate fhould refort to the Stage. Before this Law, 'twas an antient Cuftom in *Athens,* that none fhould be admitted upon the Stage, but thofe who fhould fing and utter honeft things, left the beholding immodeft Actions might draw 'em on to Vice.

IT's readily acknowledg'd that the Stage had been encourag'd by 'em, but they paid dear for their Sports, which in the Iffue proved the Ruin of their Government ; as *Juftin* obferves, who tells us that the Expence of the Stage, their Effeminacy, their fauntring at the Play-Houfe, and minding the *Performances of Poets more than the Feats of War,* made them an eafy Prey to their Enemies. *In Segnitiem diffoluti——Theatra celebrant——frequentius Scænam quam Caftra vifentes. Cap.* vi. *ad finem.*

MR. COLLIER's Adverfary frankly owns there was once a total Suppreffion (or Abdication, as he calls it) of Comedy and Tragedy at *Athens. Survey, p.* 61.

THE

THE truth is, the *Athenians*, who had been long be-witched with Plays, finding at laſt how fatal the Encou-ragement given the Stage had been to them, did not only abandon them as pernicious Evils, but condemned them by a Law, that made Actors infamous.

2. THE *Lacedemonians* would not allow of the Stage in *Sparta*, upon any Condition whatever.

PLUTARCH, who commends this People for their Senſe and Wiſdom, calls them a *Nation of Philoſophers*; no doubt of it, but they loved Diverſions as well as their Neighbours, but had no Palate for the Buffoonery of the Stage, as fore-ſeeing the Luxury of the Drama would debauch their Youth, as it did thoſe of *Athens*.

ACCORDING to *Valerius Maximus*, the *Spartans* were the neareſt to the Gravity of the *Romans* ; and, while they con-tinued obedient to the Laws of *Lycurgus*, would not ſuffer their Citizens to behold the Delicacies of *Aſia*, leſt they ſhould degenerate into a voluptuous Life. *Cap. 6. Vid. Plut. Lac. Inſtit. D. Halicarn. Antiq. Rom. l. vii. cap. 9.*

WHEN a *Rhodian* Ambaſſador demanded of a *Lacedemo-nian*, What was the Cauſe of their ſtrict Laws againſt Stage-Players? He anſwer'd, Becauſe they are hurtful to the Commonwealth——

3. THE *Maſſilians*, who were remarkable for good Diſci-pline, would not allow or tolerate any Stage-Plays in their Country.

THE Reaſon why the *Maſſilian* Republick refuſed to ad-mit them, was, becauſe the Subject of thoſe Diverſions was Intrigue and Debauchery, conſiſting generally in Relations of Adulteries, by which the Morals of the People were cor-rupted. *Val. Maxim. l. 2. c. vi.*

THE Government foreſeeing the Conſequence of ſuch Sports, and how the Infection would ſpread from Fiction in-to Practice, (that is, how the Cuſtom of beholding would beget a Cuſtom of committing the Crime) would not ſuffer thoſe Strong-Holds of Darkneſs to be erected in their Domi-nions.

4. THE *Romans*, who at firſt encouraged the Stage, lived to repent of it.

THAT Diverſion was ſubject to various Viciſſitudes among them. Before *Julius Cæſar*'s time, they ſtopt the building of a Theatre, as apprehending that the Entertainments of the Play-houſe would bring in foreign Vice, and that the old *Roman* Virtue would be loſt, and the Spirit of the People

emaſculated

emafculated and foftened ; therefore that wife Nation made the Function of Players fcandalous, feized their Freedoms, and threw them out of their Privileges, as degenerating from the Nobility and Virtue of their Anceftors. *Vid. Occa- fional Pap.* Vol. III. Numb. IX.

THE Defender of the Stage againft Mr. *Collier*, cites a *Præ- terian Edict*, which runs thus : " Whoever appears on the " Stage to fpeak or act, is declared infamous." It became fo unreputable by degrees, that 'twas thrown up to the Slaves.

BUT why was the Play-houfe thus cenfured by the *Ro- mans* ? Becaufe of its Immorality. This is plain from *Tully*, as St. *Auftin* cites him ; and *Gothofred*, who calls it a fcanda- lous Profeffion. 'Twas upon this account, and not for Hire, that the Actors became infamous among the *Romans*. *Auft. de Civit. Dei, l. 2, c. 13.*

TIBERIUS, none of the beft Emperors, tho' he much de- lighted in Plays, yet at laft, by reafon of thofe great Mif- chiefs occafioned by them, did, upon the Requeft of the Senate and People, condemn all Players to the Whipping- Poft, and then banifhed them out of *Italy* as infufferable Evils. *Tacit. An. l. 1.*

LIVY tells us, That when the Theatre was building by the Cenfor's Direction, *Scipio Nafica* fpake againft it, in the Senate-houfe, as an ufelefs, yea a debauching Experiment, and got an Act for pulling it down : *Inutile & nociturum mo- ribus. L. 48. Ep.*

DOMITIAN the Emperor, forbid all publick Players and Actors of Interludes. *Suet. in vit.*

VALERIUS MAXIMUS gives the Reafon why the Actors of the *Fabulæ Attellanæ* had better Quarter than the reft of the Players, *viz.* becaufe the Performance was more clean and inoffenfive, formed, as *Cafaubon* obferves, upon the Mo- defty of the old Satire, and was much more merry than mad. *Lib. ii.*

THIS Staunchnefs skreened the Actors from Difgrace, and purchafed their Patent of Indemnity. While the Stage countenanced Virtue, 'twas entitled to the Protection of the State ; but when it grew diffolute and impudent, the Go- vernment, to prevent the Propagation of Vice, fuppreffed it.

AUGUSTUS, who, at firft, very much delighted in Stage- Plays, having obferved the fatal Effects of them, ordered the Players to be whipped, and afterwards exiled, as in- tolerable Plagues to a State ; (particularly *Stephanio*, fome call

call him *Epiphanius*.) *Hylas & Pylas, Suet. Octav. Amsterd.*
CIↃ.IↃC.LXIII. *Sect.* 45. *pag.* 82, 83.

NERO, who doated so much upon Plays, and, to his eter‐
nal Dishonour, sometimes play d the Actor himself, saw just
Reason, before he dy'd, to turn them, and all Theatrical
Interludes, out of *Rome* and *Italy. Suet. in vita.*

YEA *Julian* himself, that vile Apostate, had so much
Goodness left in him as to prohibite Stage-Plays. In his
Epistle to *Arsacius,* the Pagan High-Priest of *Galatia,* he for‐
bid all the *Gentile* Priests, and their People, to frequent
the Play-house. *Sozom. Eccl. Hist. Paris. 1668. cap.* 16.

TRAJAN the Emperor put down the Stage, and banished
the Actors; of which memorable Act *Pliny* II. speaks. *Plin.
Sec. Panegyr. Trajano, dict. Colon. Allobr. p.* 38.

ANTONINUS PIUS was favourable to them; but his Suc‐
cessor *M. Aurelius Antoninus,* in order to regulate Manners,
took the Players with him to the War, and, by an Edict,
forbad all publick Plays at *Rome* and *Antioch;* but that not
meeting with the expected Success, he banished all Stage-
Players as Corrupters of the Empire, loaded three Ships
with them which he sent to the Governor of the *Hellespont,*
to be put into the House of Correction.

THE Christian Emperors were as remarkable in their Op‐
position to the Stage

CONSTANTINE the Great, first Christian Emperor, born
and bred in *Britain,* did, by an Edict, abolish Plays, and
all other obscene Customs of the *Gentiles. Euseb. in Vita So‐
zom. Hist. Eutrop.*

THEODOSIUS the Great suppressed Play-houses, as the
Fountains and Nurseries of all Wickedness in Cities, and ba‐
nished all Players, Singers, and Women-Dancers, by a pub‐
lick Edict; as *Chrysostom* relates,——*Nequitiæ fontes exclusit
& subvertit?*——*hinc*——*Nequitiæ radices in Civitate germinave‐
runt*——*Homil.* 17. *ad Populum Antioch.*

VALENTINIAN, and *Gratian,* and *Valens* the Emperor,
made publick Laws against Stage-Plays and common Actors.
Codex Theodos. l. 15. *de Spectac.*

THUS we see the Stage condemned by Pagan and Christian
Emperors.

5. SALVIAN tells us, That Plays were not acted in
many Cities of *Gaul* and *Spain,* nor in all the Cities of the
Romans.

6. THE *Goths,* and other Barbarians censured and con‐
demned Stage-Plays as effeminate and ridiculous Super‐
fluities.

7. THE

7. THE old *Germans*, who are noted for their ſtriƈt regards to Chaſtity, were not corrupted with the Allurements of Plays, and Shews, as *Tacitus* tells us, *De Morib. Germ. Vid. Cluver.*

8. PLAYS are condemned by the Laws, tho encouraged by the People of *England*.

I SHALL look no farther back than King *Henry* VIII's time, when there was an Aƈt made againſt Mummers ; by which the Players were fined and impriſoned for three Months: the Penalty for ſelling Vizors, or keeping them in the Houſe, is Twenty Shillings for every Vizor. 3 *H.* VIII. *cap.* 9. *&* 3

IN Qu. *Elizabeth's* Reign the Play-houſes in *Grace-Church-ſtree:*, on *Ludgate-Hill*, *White-Friars*; &c. were pulled down, and Stage-Plays driven out of the City: *Whetſton's Mirrour for Maiyſtrates.* By a Statute made in the 39th of her Reign, all Tinkers, Pedlars, Players of Interludes, unleſs autho-riz'd by Barons, were accounted Rogues, and to be whipt. *An.* 39 *Eliz. See An.* 1mo *Jacobi* I. *c.* vii.

BY a Statute in King *James's* Reign; there is a Penalty of 10 *l.* laid upon thoſe, who, in any Stage-Plays, Interludes, May-Games, Shews, and ſuch like, did jeſtingly, or pro-fanely, ſpeak or uſe the Holy Name of God, or of Chriſt, or of the Holy Ghoſt. *Ann.* 3 *Jac.* I. *c.* 21.

'TIS true, King *James* publiſh'd a Book of Sports, and 'tis as true he wiſh'd it burnt before he dy'd.

THESE Aƈts of Parliament were reviv'd and inforc'd in the 12th of Queen *Anne*, by which Players of Interludes are to be puniſhed as Rogues: The Conſtable, and other Inhabi-tants may bring them before a Juſtice ; Officers, negleƈting their Duty, forfeit Twenty Shillings.

How vile then muſt theſe Players be, that are vomited out by Church and State ? In the Year 1697. by order of the *French* King, the *Italian* Players were expelled the King-dom ; and I very well remember, that in 1703. the *French* Stage lay under Excommunication. The Theatres alſo have, ſome time ago, been ſhut up by the Pope, and in the Terri-tories of *Brandenburgh* by the King of *Pruſſia* ; and ſeveral *Eu-ropean* Countries would never endure them in any Form, or under any Regulation. I'll conclude this Head with the *Jews.*

9. IN the Opinion of *Joſephus* and *Maccabees*, Stage-Plays were direƈtly oppoſite to the Laws, Governments, Rites, and Cuſtoms of the *Jews* ; therefore they did not only oppoſe *Herod*.

Herod, but confpired his Death, when he introduced among them Plays and Shews in honour of *Auguftus*. *Antiq. Jud. l. 15. c. 11.* The *Maccabees* inform us, That *Jafon*, and his bafe Confederates, were the firft that brought in thefe Plays among the *Jews*: 1 *Maccab.* 1. 2 *Maccab.* 4. & *cap.* 6.

PHILO-JUDÆUS, a very learned *Jew*, who flourifhed in the Apoftles times, condemns Stage-Plays as vain and hurtful Paftimes, in which Thoufands miferably fpend their Time, and wafte their Lives; ἐπεὶ πόϑεν ἀλλοϑεν——*De Agricultura. Opera, Francf.* CIƆ.IƆC.XCI. (*p.*192. *B. c.*)

STAGE-PLAYS *are no where authoriz'd or allow'd by the Church of* England *as fuch, but every where condemned by the Purity of her Doctrine, and by fome of her moft eminent Lights.*

NONE of her Articles, Canons, or Homilies, give the leaft Encouragement to thofe ludicrous Sports; or any other Diverfions that recommend themfelves by indecent Levity; But, on the contrary, in conformity to the Statutes of the Land, and Practice of the Primitive Church, condemns all kinds of unlawful Sports, as appears by her Canons, Catechifm, and Univerfities, as well as by fome of her moft eminent Members.

1. BY one of her Canons, no Clergyman fhall fpend his time idly by Day or Night, playing at *Dice, Cards, or Tables*, or any other unlawful Game; which includes Mummeries and Interludes, according to the Statutes. *Can.* 75.

2. THE Church-Catechifm, in renouncing the *Pomps* and *Vanities* of this World, feems to refer to thefe Theatrical Shews, that are fome of thofe things we renounce in Baptifm; becaufe, in this Senfe, the antient Church underftood thefe words which we borrow from them.

THE Primitive Chriftians abftain'd from Stage-Plays; becaufe they look'd upon them to be fome of thofe *Pomps* and *Vanities* which they had renounc'd in their Baptifm.

THUS St. *Cyril*, by Pomps, underftands the Sights and Sports of the Theatre, and fuch like Vanities. *Catech. Myft.*

TERTULLIAN, *Cyprian*, St. *Auftin*, &c. remonftrated againft the Stage, becaufe the frequenting of it was an abjuring their Abjuration of the Pomps of this World in their Baptifm. *De Spectac.*

THE Fathers, who liv'd near the Apoftolical Times, knew beft what was underftood by this Baptifmal Renunciation; and they fay, Stage-Plays were particularly included in it:

D

and

and if fo, then it will follow, that our Attendance upon the Stage is a practical Renunciation of our Baptifm.

So far as we countenance thefe impure Scenes, fo far we enter into a League with the Flefh and the Devil againft Chrift. Do but take a View, fays Dr. *Horneck*, of the Writings of the Primitive Fathers, and you'll find them unanimous in this Affertion, *viz.* That in our Baptifm, when we renounce the Devil and his Works, the Pomps and Glory of the World, we do. particularly renounce Stage-Plays, and fuch ludicrous Reprefentations. *P.* 225. *of his* Sirenes.

' How, fays *Salvian*, do we pretend to worfhip God in the
' Church, when we are continually ferving the Devil in
' thofe obfcene Plays? When we are in the Theatre, do we
' follow the Steps of Chrift? What Folly is this? What
' can't we have a conftant Scene of Merriment and Laughter,
' unlefs we make our Mirth and Joy become a Sin? What
' can't we be merry without being wicked, or ufe our Mirth
' without affronting our Maker? for, in the publick Shews,
' there is a kind of Apoftacy from the Faith, and a mortal
' Prevarication about the bleffed Sacraments.'

' ' THE firft thing Chriftians do in their Baptifm, is to re-
' nounce the Devil, his Pomps, Shews, and Works; and
' therefore thefe Pomps and Shews, according to our own
' Profeffion, are the Works of the Devil.' *Salvian*; *In Spectaculis enim quædam Apoftafia Fidei*, *p.* 196, 197, *&* 193. *Spectacula & Pompæ etiam juxta noftram Profeffionem Opera funt
Diaboli*——*p.* 193, 196, 197.

' How *(adds he)* dareft thou, Oh Chriftian, run from
' Church, a holy Place, to the Stage, the Synagogue of Sa-
' tan? How dareft thou go to a Play-houfe after Baptifm,
' when thou haft confefs'd thofe very Plays to be the Works
' of the Devil? Thou haft renounced the Devil, and all his
' pompous Shews; fo that by attending thefe, you return
' to the Devil'——*Oh Chriftiane! Spectacula poft Baptifmum*——
Ibid. p. 197, 198.

3. OUR Univerfities, in the days of their Purity, paft the fame Cenfure upon Plays.

MR. STEPHEN GOSSON tells us, That upon his own Knowledge (*A. D.* 1581.) many famous Men of both Univerfities had made open Outcries againft the Inconveniences bred by Plays, and that they were of Opinion, they ought not to be fuffer'd in a Chriftian Commonwealth. *His Plays confuted,
Act.* 5.

DR.

Dr. Reynolds affirms, That the beft and graveft Divines in the Univerfity of *Oxford*, condemned Stage-Plays, by an exprefs Statute made in a full Convocation of the whole Univerfity in the Year 1584. whereby the ufe of all common Plays was exprefly prohibited in the Univerfity, left the younger fort (who are prone to imitate all kind of Vice) being Spectators of fo many leud and evil Sports as in them are practis'd, fhould be corrupted by them. *His Overthrow of Stage-Plays, p.* 151, 153.

And, he adds, I have read of a Statute enacted at *Cambridge*, that no common Actors fhould be fuffer'd to play within the Precincts of the Univerfity, for fear they fhould debauch the Students Manners.

Obj. The Univerfities allow the Scholars to act.

Anfw. Private Interludes are tolerated. In times of Popery, fome particular Statutes were made, that requir'd *Latin* Comedies, for Learning-fake only; but I have not feen any publick Approbation of Stage-Plays by the Univerfities.

4. In the next Place we are to confider the Judgment of eminent Churchmen about Stage-Plays.

We may know the Thoughts of the Church by her Sons, who generally look upon the Diverfions of the Stage as very pernicious Entertainments. I'll begin with,

[1.] Dr. Parker, Archbifhop of *Canterbury*, who condemns Plays in his Book *de Antiq. Eccl. Brit.* 1572.

[2.] Dr. G. Alley, Bifhop of *Exeter*, and Divinity-Lecturer at St. *Paul's*, in the fecond Year of Queen *Elizabeth*, does, in his Book, called, *The Poor Man's Library*, declare, with great warmth, againft Stage-Plays, as the Fuel of Luft, Occafion of Adultery, and other intolerable Evils. *Lond.* 1571.

[3.] Dr. Beard of *Huntingdon*, and Dr. *Taylor*, the famous Preacher of *Aldermanbury*, fpeaking of Plays and Comedies, and fuch like May-Games, fay, *They have no other Ufe but to deprave and corrupt Good-Manners, and open a Door to all Uncleannefs*——*The Holy Scripture is often by thefe filthy Swine prophan'd*——*Theatre of God's Judgments, Edit.* 4. *Lond.* 1648. *cap.* 36.

[4.] Lord Chief Justice Hale, who was fo great an Ornament to the Bench, advifes his Son thus : ' Let your Re' creations be healthy and creditable, without too much ' Time or Money ; go not to Stage-Plays——3*d Ep. to one of his Sons, p.* 273, 275.

[5.] ARCHBISHOP USHER, the Glory of the Church, speaking of Interludes and Stage-Plays, says, They offend against the seventh Commandment in several Instances—— Besides, the Wantonnefs therein us'd in Attire, Speech and Action ; the Man puts on the Woman's Apparel (which is forbidden as a thing abominable, *Deut.* 22. 5.) much Filthinefs is prefented to the Beholders, and foolifh Talking and Jefting, which are not convenient. Fornication and all Uncleannefs (which ought not to be once nam'd among Chriftians) is made a Spectacle of Joy and Laughter, *Eph.* 5. 3, 4. therefore they who go to fee fuch Sights, and hear fuch Words, fhew their Neglect of Chriftian Duty, and Careleffnefs in Sinning, whenas they willingly commit themfelves into the Snare of the Devil. *Body of Div. Edit.* 1. *in* 4*to, Lond. A. D.* 1702.

;[6.] DR. BRAY, writing upon this Subject, says, As to *Pomps*, the Antients meant by them thofe pompous Spectacles, Plays, and Scenical Reprefentations exhibited in the *Roman* Theatres ; which becaufe they were fo leud, cruel, and impious, the Primitive Bifhops and Fathers of the Church ftrictly enjoin'd all Chriftians, at their Baptifm, not to frequent, or fo much as to be once prefent, or ever feen at them.

OUR modern Plays are no lefs inferiour to the antient ones in Impiety and Leudnefs, than they are in Shew and Pompoufnefs ; and having fuch a malignant Influence on Faith and Manners, as is own'd by almoft all Perfons, they ought never to be frequented by Chriftians ; and it may be very well look'd upon as a Breach of your Baptifmal Vow, for any of you to be hereafter prefent at them. *His Difcourfe of the Baptifmal Covenant, p.* 118.

[7.] DR. HORNECK, who has writ againft Plays, says—— Actor and Spectator go away from the Theatre worfe than they came; and tho both come away laughing, yet both prepare for bitter Mourning and Lamentation. The Plays, *adds he,* we fpeak of, are fuited to the loofe Humour of the Age, which feems to hate all things that are ferious, and delights in nothing fo much as in Jefts and Fooleries, and feeing the moft venerable things turn'd into Ridicule——No Play relifhes but what is ftuffed with Love-Tricks ; and hat which makes People laugh moft, is the beft Comedy. *His Letter againft Plays in his Book on Judgment.*

[8.] DR. TILLOTSON, late *Archbifhop of Canterbury,* that Star of the firft Magnitude in the Firmament of the Church, speaking

speaking of some Parents, says, They are such Monsters, I had almost said Devils, as not to know how to give good things to their Children——Instead of bringing them to God's Church, they bring them to the Devil's Chapels, to Play-houses, and Places of Debauchery, those Schools and Nurseries of Leudness and Vice. *Serm.* 3. *Education of Children, Lond.* 1694. *Edit.* 2. *p.* 153, 154.

[9.] DR. JOHN EDWARDS, in his *Preacher*, speaking of those who preach at Court and great Cities, says, They can't shew themselves faithful in their Office, unless they dissuade their Hearers from frequenting of Play-houses. He adds, That the Entertainments of the Stage, as they are manag'd and us'd, have a natural and unavoidable Tendency to that which is sinful and unlawful ; for they foment Idleness, and profuse wasting of precious Time : They dissolve the Spirits into Lightness and Wantonness ; they foster Immodesty and Obscenity ; they nourish Licentiousness and Debauchery ; they encourage Profaneness, the Youth especially of both Sexes are corrupted and ruined by these publick Shews, and almost every day affords us some Proof of it.

IN short, if your Auditors be addicted to Plays, they'll not care for your Sermons, unless your Sermons be a-kin to the Plays. *Preacher, Part* I. *pag.* 100, 101. *printed* 1705. *Edit.* 2.

IN another place he calls the Play-houses Shops of Impiety and Impudence, Schools of Obscenity. *Preacher, Part* III. *p.* 188, 189.

[10.] DR. FOG, late Dean of *Chester*, saith, That if the Stage be not purged from that Filthiness both of Speech and Gesture, which is usually represented there, we must join with the antient Fathers, and civilized Heathens, in condemning it ; for considering who they are that become the usual Spectators of such Wickedness, they are Incentives to the corrupt Nature of the Beholders, who can't see wanton Actions so lively represented, but have those Affections moved, which have neither Grace nor Virtue enough to make the best use of what they see, any more than others can walk on hot Coals, and their Feet not be burnt ; or handle Pitch, and their Fingers not be defiled. *His two Treatises, printed at* Chester, 1712. *p.* 153.

[11.] DR. KENNETT, the present Bishop of *Peterborough*, speaking of 41, says,——It seems very evident, that the Liberty and Delight then taken in Plays and Operas, did sadly corrupt the Minds and Manners of our People, and so

les

let in that Loofenefs and Irreligion, which ferv'd to fuggeft the Wickednefs and Villanies foon after acted in the Civil War.

[12.] To crown all, Queen *Anne*, Head of the Church, fupprefs'd, in her Reign, thofe Seminaries of Hell, called, *May-Fair*, *Bartholomew*, and *Southwark-Fairs*, where Multitudes were annually debauched by the profane Plays acted there. I might add more ; but if they'll not hear thefe good Men, who fpeak the Language of Reafon, and the Univerfal Church, neither will they be perfuaded tho one rofe from the Dead.

VI.

AMONG *the Papifts, who have almoft converted all Religion into Plays, are found Enemies to the Stage,* upon the fcore of its Profanenefs.

BEFORE the Reformation in *England*, nothing more common than Interludes and Comedies, form'd upon religious Subjects ; and thefe were acted even in confecrated Places, as appears by Statutes made againft fuch Practiees: nor are they yet cured of this Evil, as is evident by the News from *Oporto* in *Portugal* ; where, on the 13th of *February*, 1720-1. an *Opera* was perform'd, in which were reprefented the Nativity of Chrift, and the principal Occurrences fince the Creation,

Now tho the Papifts are as much addicted to Plays as any, and the Jefuits have often acted the Paffion of Chrift inftead of Preaching it ; yet their learned Writers, and Defenders of the Church, condemn Stage-Plays, as injurious to Religion and Government.

MARIANA, the Jefuit, has writ one entire Treatife againft Stage-Plays, calling the Stage the Shop of Uncleannefs, and a Plague fatal to Kingdoms. *Officina Impudicitiæ, Exitiale malum Reipub. de Spectac.* With whom agrees *Matthew Paris*, a famous *Englifh* Hiftorian.

CARDINAL BARONIUS fpeaks againft them in his Ecclefiaftical Annals.

CARDINAL BELLARMINE cenfures Plays as unchriftian Paftimes.

ONUPHRIUS PAN. VERONENSIS, after having related the idolatrous Pagan Original of Plays, condemns them, quoting St. *Cyprian* and *Tertullian* againft them. *De Ludis Circen. Venet.* 1600. *l.* 1. *c.* 1. *&c.*

JULIUS CÆSAR BULINGERUS has writ an excellent Treatife againft all kinds of Stage-Plays, proving them to be utterly unlawful.

HENRICUS SPONDANUS proves, That Stage-Plays were always condemned by the Primitive Chriftians as the Pomps of the Devil. *Epit. Baron. Mogun.* 1614.

NICOLAUS DE CLEMANGIS reckons Stage-Plays among the Diforders in his time. *De nov. celeb. non inftituendis, Lugd. Bat.*

IF Number would add to the Strength of an Argument, I could multiply Authors from this Quarter, and fummon in *Anfelm, Aquinas, Gratian,* and others; but thefe are fufficient to prove, that even in the Church of *Rome,* where Religion is metamorphos'd into Pageantry and pompous Reprefentations, fome of her greateft and beft Men have damned the Stage as the Angel of the bottomlefs Pit, whofe Name is *Apollyon.*

AND fhall Proteftants, Members of the Reformed Body, patronize a corrupt Stage? When Papifts, Members of the Mafs-houfe, declare againft it as the Corrupter of all Religion? .Tell it not in *Gath,* publifh it not in the Streets of *Afkelon,* left the Daughters of the *Philiftines* rejoice, and the Uncircumcifed triumph, when they hear how Reformers have exchang'd the Superftitions of *Rome* for the Vices of the Stage.

VII.

FROM the whole I obferve, *Tho there may be an innocent Reprefentation of Perfons and Actions in a Dramatick Way; yet Play-houfes, as they have been, and now generally are managed, ought not to be frequented by Chriftians.*

IN the precedent Pages, you have feen the Stage arraigned and condemned by the concurrent Teftimonies of fober Heathens, *Jews,* wife States, Chriftians, both Antient and Modern, Proteftant and Popifh.

You have heard their repeated and loud Exclamations againft it, as a Practice pernicious to the common Interefts of Mankind; and no wonder, when indeed moft of the Theatrick Compofitions are little elfe than a bold Confpiracy againft Reafon and Religion.

FOR here the Bounds between Virtue and Vice are broken down, facred things are not fpared, if they ferve to make up the Decorum of the Act, or to furnifh out an obfcene Droll. In thefe Shews our Holy Religion has often

been

been made the Subject of Ridicule, and sometimes even in
the Character and Habit of a Clergyman; an Evil com-
plain d of in the eighth General Council, *viz. That then
'twas a Custom, in the Courts of Princes, to clothe Laymen in
Episcopal Robes, who both in Tonsure, and other Ornaments,
should act a Bishop's Part, and likewise to make a ridiculous Patriarch, with whom they might sport themselves; and is condemned by Can. 16.——— Laicum insignib. Episcopalib. qui &
Tonjura——— & c easse ridiculum Patriarcham quo se oblecta-
rent. Caranza.*

No wonder the Sacred Priesthood could not escape their
Taunts, when the Holy Scripture itself has been burlesqued
and turned into Travesty; and, to this day, no Diversions
more common in some Country-Places than Interludes,
wherein a mock History of the Bible is frequently given:
In the first Act of the Play, called, *Mock-Astrologer,* the
Scene is a Chapel, and the Time is taken up in ridiculing
Devotion.

But supposing that the Ambassadors of Heaven had a
Protection from the Stage; yet this gay and soft way of
living is inconsistent with the Maxims of that Religion;
which obliges us to crucify the Flesh, with its Lusts and Affections, and to turn away our Eyes from beholding Vanity.
Nay, there can't be a more ready way to introduce universal Libertinism, to baffle pious Inclinations, and to banish
even common Morality out of the World; than by encou-
raging Play-houses, those common Nests of Rakes, Bullies,
and Wantons, where Vices are represented in jest, and afterwards practis'd in good earnest. When Vice is dressed up
in its Gaieties, and represented in all its Allurements, it in-
sensibly insinuates itself into the unwary Mind, and soon
renders insipid all the Entertainments of Virtue; yea, the
scandalous and impudent Gestures of the Actors, convey
the Poison with greater force than their infectious Tongues;
and yet so intoxicated are Men with these Theatrical Diver-
tisements, that they are preferred to those of the Temple.

This was the Complaint of *Salvian,* that holy Bishop,
viz. 'That Men preferred Plays before the Churches of
' God, despised the Altar, and honoured the Theatres. If,
' *says he,* it happens, as it oft does on the same day, that
' there is a Church Festival, and publick Plays, which of
' the two Places has the greatest Congregation, the Temple
' or the Theatre? Which are most crowded, the Pews in
' the Church, or Seats in the Play-house?———

' I

nt, *contrived on purpose for the more effectual Propa-*
the Works of Darkness.

firſt uſe of the Maſque is referred by *Horace* to *Æſ-*
whereas before the Actors had no other Diſguiſe,
aub their Faces with odd Colours, and that was well
when the Stage was no better than a Cart.

as common with Pagans, in their Solemnities and
s, to honour their Idols with Plays, and Dances, and
Poſtures; hence it is we read of their dancing Prieſts,
orybantes, Salii, Curetes.

Corybantes were the Prieſts of *Cybele*, who, in their
Proceſſions, danced, and are deſcribed by *Lucretius,*
, &c.

Salii (who had their Names from *Saliendo*) were
ſts of *Mars*, who, on the ſolemn days of *Cybele, Bac-*
cus, &c. performed their Devotions with Dancings, in
and Manner of our Morris-Dances and Maſquerade-
hat are a Scandal in their Nature, and Poiſon in their
ation.

BIUS tells us, That after the *Arcadian* Children had
ſtructed in the Muſick of *Philoxenus* and *Timotheus,*
re brought early to the Theatre, where they cele-
he Feaſts of *Bacchus* with Songs and Dances. B. IV.

old *Romans* ſurrounded the Altars with devotional
: Thus they kept their *Saturnalia* for ſeven days to-
which they ſpent in Dancing, Feaſting, Plays, and
les; wherein Maſters and Servants were hail Fellow
t, and all Perſons and Things common.

he end of this Feſtival they celebrated their *Feſtum*
rium, on *January* I. in honour of *Janus.* The Solem-
s obſerved with Stage-Plays, *Mummeries, Masks, Danc-*
here a boundleſs Liberty was uſed by the Company.
the black Original we tranſcribe in our Maſque-

s the *Greeks* kept their *Saturnalia,* and other ſolemn
s, with *Miſques* and Dancings; where the utmoſt In-
e was given to criminal Paſſions; no wonder, ſince
en Religion was in a great meaſure a Myſtery of Iniqui-
dneſs was conſecrated in the Temples, as well as practiſed.
ews: 'Tis not therefore ſtrange, that the Stage ſhould
ome of the Liberties of their Theology.

RDING to *Polydore Virgil, Mummings, Maſquerades,*
uiſes, uſed in *England,* came from the Feaſt of *Pal-*

las,

'IF there happen to be any Feaſts of the Church, they,
'who call themſelves Chriſtians, don't only forbear the
'Church, but, if they are in it, immediately run out, if
'they hear there are Plays acted. They leave Chriſt on
'the Altar, that they may feed their Eyes that go a who-
'ring after thoſe unclean Sights.' *Salvian. de Gubern. Dei, pag.*
200.

BUT no Perſons ſo ſuſceptible of the Infection as young
ones, who, from a natural Vivacity of Imagination, hate
the Fatigue of Buſineſs, and therefore are ſoon taken with
that ſort of idle Life; theſe therefore ought to be effectually caution'd againſt the Contagion of the Stage.

CHILDREN, who are the hopes of a Nation, merit our
ſtricteſt Regards: a Neglect in their Education is an Error
in the firſt Concoction. *Pythagoras,* in his Speech to Children, obſerves,

'THEY are the deareſt to the Gods, for which reaſon
'they were employ'd to pray to the Gods for Rain in a
'time of Scarcity; that they only, being always ſanctify'd,
'had leave to live in the Temple; that the *Pythian, Ne-*
'*mean,* and *Iſthmian Games* were inſtituted for their ſakes.
'*Apollo* and *Cupid,* the kindeſt to Men of all the Gods, were
'always repreſented as Boys, by reaſon of the Sanctity of
'that Age.' *See his Life.*

To ſum up all; To attend theſe ludicrous and obſcene
Shews, and take pleaſure in them, is unbecoming the Man,
the Gentleman, and the Chriſtian.

How unbecoming the Dignity of a rational Nature, to
act the Part of a Buffoon, or to be pleas'd with thoſe
who do ſo? What Violence does he offer to the Reaſon
of Mankind, who repreſents Vice as faſhionable and gen-
teel? and what a ſorry mean Soul actuates that Man, who
makes theſe ludicrous Actions the Ingredients of his Pleaſure? 'Tis this Meanneſs of Spirit that fills the Grand Sig-
nior's Court with ſo many Mutes, Tumblers, Dwarfs, Buffoons——By theſe ſordid and fooliſh Sports the Muſſulmen
grow effeminate, and unfit for Arms and Embaſſies.

WHAT a Diminution to the Honour of Gentlemen (who
by Birth are deſign'd for Offices of State) to go to Chil-
drens Play, at the Expence of ſo much Time and Money,
and all for the Diverſion of a little Laughter, rais'd by Buffoons, Vagabonds, Jeſters, Strollers, Dancers, Fidlers, Players, who go about to poiſon the Minds and Morals of the Nation,

tion, and to teach People to whore and swear the shortest way?

WHAT a pretty Figure does my Gentleman make, when he stands bareheaded before a Pack of Scoundrel Actors, who are infamous by the Laws of the *Gentiles*, as well as those of *England*, and whose Office at best, is only to excite rude and excessive Mirth, and clownish Laughter in the Audience, without the least Pretence to moral Instruction?

GENTLEMEN generally are, or should be, Men of Politeness and good Taste; how ridiculous is it to see these mix with the Dregs of the People, who have no relish of Decency and Honour in their Rustick Acclamations? How awkward a Figure does the grinning Gentleman make, when the Modesty of his Lady (and all her Sex) is attack'd by impudent Actors?

To see the Christian in the Play-house, that Conventicle of Vice, is yet more shocking. What thou a Christian, and a Spectator of those wanton Postures and Actions that constitute the greatest part of some Plays? What thou a Christian, a Member of the Church, and frequent the Play-house, that School of Darkness, and usual Rendevouz of Debauchees? With what Pleasure can Ladies and Gentlemen of Virtue associate with these?

WITH what face dare you behold the Holy Temple, who defile your Eyes with being Spectators of vain and wanton Shews? With what Conscience can you approach the sacred Table one day, and run to a Play-house the next day, where the Entertainment is *Smut*; or as the *Tatler*, a Friend of the Play-house, speaks, *immodest Action, empty Show, or impertinent Activity.*

THUS I have briefly accounted for the Conduct and Treatment of the Stage, where you have the Substance of what others have deliver'd upon the Subject more at large; as *Prynn*, in his *Histrio-Mastix*, *Collier's three Treatises, Horneck's Letter, Occasional Paper*. In short,

IF those who'll vouchsafe to give these Anti-theatrical Arguments the reading, see no weight in them, I must despair of their Conviction, till this flagrant Instance or Vanity ends in Vexation of Spirit.

BEFORE I conclude, I shall add a few Reflections upon Masquerades, those unhallow'd Groves of Immorality. This Entertainment, so fatal to Virtue and Principles of Honour,

Honour, has infected our High-Plac Favourite-Diversion of the Times; timely Redress of this Grievance, th try, I fear, will soon metamorphose *Sodom* for Lewdness.

THE *Churches may e'en be shut up, open*; yea, and the Poets too must its time obtains the universal vogue; ments of the Masque will soon rend Performance of the Poet.

THE Pagan Plays were not altoge Modern, and the Modern Plays are compar'd with the Masquerades, tha Dregs of Baseness, and sink the Hor to the lowest Ebb of Infamy.

IN order to regale and heighten th sume variety of Forms; the Gen the Dress of a Woman, the Gentle Habit of Men. This is (as *Ben John* leaping from the Stage to the Tumb Wit to the original Dung-Cart.

BEING thus equipp'd, the Farce work, and every body may be as le Oh! who can proceed and describe tremble? Who can think of the vil tions made there, without being sei

NOT long since a certain Gent those Plays, debauch'd his own D Mask was thrown off, and she appe what Rage, Vexation, and Anguish Father, who liv'd under horrible C and at last died with Horror.

IN order to give the common these Masquerades, I'll briefly enq and the Sentiments of Heathens ab how they (and their Concomitant only by the Laws of the Land, b and Nature.

THE Original of Masquerades, wit formance, by Masks, mixed Dancings or rather this kind of Pastime may *las*, which was celebrated with *Vizors* and *painted Visages*, named *Quinquatria* of the *Romans*. ' As for Masques, *says* ' *he*, they are so devilish, that no Honesty can be pretended ' to colour them.' *De Invent. Rerum.*

THESE *Quinquatrial Feasts* were like to those the *Athenians* called *Panathenæa*, Feasts celebrated in honour of *Minerva*, where there was usually a *Chorus* of young Men and Women that danced.

THUS we have traced the *Masquerades* to their Fountainhead : they were invented by Heathens in honour of their false Gods, but among Christians how is the true God dishonoured, by the promiscuous Congress of Masqueraders, whose nocturnal Revels, if not restrained, will prove more fatal to Religion, than the Villany of the *South-Sea* Directors has been to the National Credit ?

BY this ludicrous Pastime the Heathens pretended to pay their Devoirs to the Gods : On the other hand, Christians turn it into a Scene of sinful Merriment. We borrow this pompous Diversion from Pagans, and, in the acting of it, we are worse than Pagans. With these Plays they pleased the Devil, we affront God with them; theirs was Devotion, ours *Rebellion*. The Heathens more excusable : their Deities were great Examples of Vice, and worshipped by their own Inclinations; but the Christian Religion is quite of another Complexion, forbids the remotest Tendencies to Evil; that which might pass for Entertainment in Heathenism, is detestable in Christianity.

II.

THOUGH *the Practice of Masquerading, with the Concomitant of it, viz. amorous and mixed Dancing, was invented by the Heathens, yet was condemned by the wiser sort of them, as well as by the Christian Church.*

AMONG the *Romans*, common Dancing was counted a Badge of Dishonesty; and yet, according to *Macrobius*, they were not able to secure their Daughters against the Infection of the Dancing-School.

SCIPIO AFRICANUS ÆMILIUS, in his Speech against the Judiciary Law of *Tiberius Gracchus*, says, That those who frequented the Dancing-School, were taught dishonest Arts.

CICERO, by way of Contempt (stiles *Gabinius, Catiline's* Consul) a Dancer, accuses *Verres* for his intimate Acquaintance

tance with *Aproneus*, a great Dancer. He cenfures *Cato* for
ftiling *L. Muræna*, a *Roman* Conful, a Dancer; for, fays
he, no fober Man will dance, if he be not diftracted.

In his, Oration for *D. Rege*, he takes a great deal of
pains to excufe him from the Infamy of Dancing. In his
Book of Offices, he intimates, That an honeft Man would
not dance in publick, tho he might be Heir to *Marcus Craf-
fus*, a rich *Roman* Conful. *Lib.* iii. *cap.* 19.

JUSTIN ftiles Dances the Inftruments of Luxury; *Ad-
duntur Inftrumenta Luxuriæ, Tympana & Crepundia*, *Hift.
Edit. A. D.* 1587. *lib.* 30. *pag.* 189. *Suetonius* reckons Dancing among the Vices of *Caligula* the Emperor.

EVEN their Poets cenfure Dancing as the Practice of lewd
and drunken Creatures at Feafts. *Juvenal* makes Dancing
the Character of an Adulterefs, the Fuel of Lufts, the
Caufe of Adultery, and counts him an unhappy Husband
who has a dancing Wife. *Sat.* 6. & 11.

HOMER fays, That, among other Effects of Drunkennefs, it makes a wife Man fing and dance; by which it
appears, that in thofe days it was not cuftomary for wife
Men to dance, but when they were drunk. *Odyff. vid. Virg.
Tibul. Hor.*

VENUS, faith *Polydore Virgil*, becaufe fhe alone would
not feem to be a Whore, ordained in *Cyprus*, That Women
fhould proftitute themfelves for Money, and to give the
finifhing Stroke to this Debauchery, one *Melampus* brought
out of *Egypt* into *Greece* the Rites of *Bacchus*'s Sacrifices,
wherein Men and Women herded together in the Night;
much *(adds he)* like our Shews or Dances, called Mafques or
Mafquerades in *England*. *Lib.* iii. *cap.* 12.

IT's evident from hence, that thofe Dances, which are
common among Chriftians, were odious in the Eyes of Heathens; much more would they have condemned our obfcene Dancings of Mafquerades, if they now lived. How
ftrange is it to fee Chriftians, who have happily emerged
out of Pagan Darknefs, relapfe into their grofs Errors
and Senfualities!

I Now proceed to the Primitive Fathers (and Councils)
who every where cenfure mixed Dancings; which bears fo
great a fhare in Mafquerades, either on the Stage, or elfe-
where, as the Incendiaries of Luft, and altogether unlawful:
they are too numerous to be quoted at large in fo fmall a
Compafs, therefore I fhall only refer to a few of them; as
Clemens

Clemens Alexandrinus, Arnobius adv. Gentes, Cyprian, Tertullian, Nazianzen, &c. Some of the Fathers, especially *Chryfostom, Fulgentius,* fay, The Devil himfelf, who danced in the Daughter of *Herodias,* was the Original of this lafcivious Dancing.

The *Laodicean* Council condemns Dancing at Marriages; *Non oportet Chriftianos faltare: Can.* 53. *Caranza.* The third Council of *Toledo* calls Dancing an irreligious filthy Cuftom: *Saltationibus turpibus invigilare, Can.* 22. *Caranz.* See *Concil. Agath. Conc. Arelat. Concil. Conftant. in Trull. &c.*

Christian Authors, of a more modern Date, concur with the antient Fathers and Councils, in condemning fuch Dancings as unlawful; not only Reformers from Popery, but Papifts themfelves, and all thofe who write on the feventh Commandment, as I have read or heard of. See *Alex. Alefius, Alex. Fabritius, Lud. Vives, Erafmus de Contemptu Mundi, Agrippa de Vanitate, Polyd. Virgil. de Inventione, Peter Martyr, Flaccus Illyricus, Martin Bucer, Lyra, Bullinger, Aretius, Polanus,* Dr. *Reynolds's Overthrow of the Stage,* Bifhop *Babington, Pifcator, Perkins, Downham,* Dr. *Ames, cum multis aliis.*

I shall conclude this with the *Waldenfes* and *Albigenfes,* the pureft Remains of Chriftianity, who, in their Cenfure of Dancing, fay, *That Dancing is the Devil's Proceffion, and be that enters into a Dance, enters into his Poffeffion. As many Paces as a Man makes in Dancing, fo many Paces does be make to Hell,* &c.

III.

Masquerades *are condemned by the Laws of the Land, not only after, but before the Reformation.*

To come down to our *Englifh* Conftitution: Thofe Plays are accounted dangerous, and therefore fevere Laws have been made againft the fpreading of that Infection through the Kingdom.

Thus in King *Henry* VIII's time, an Act was made, That if any Perfons did put on ftrange and antick Habits, and difguife themfelves with Vizors, and, fo difguifed, enter Houfes, to divert the People, that they fhould be arrefted as Vagabonds, and committed to the Goal for three Months without Bail, and then to be fined, at the Difcretion of the Juftices.

It is further enacted, That any Perfon, who fhould keep the faid Vizor or Vizors, fhall forfeit for every Vizor

Twenty

Twenty Two Shillings, and be imprifoned and fined by the Juftices befides. 3 *H.* VIII. *c.*9.

Since the Reformation, by the Laws of *Elizabeth*, *James*, and *Charles*. See the Statutes.

IV.

Men *putting on Womens Apparel, and Women Mens Apparel, as they do in the Mafquerades, is a Practice condemned by Revelation, and the Light of Nature.*

The Holy Scriptures tell us, *The Women fhall not wear that which pertains to the Man, neither fhall a Man put on a Woman's Garment ; for all that do fo are an Abomination to the Lord:* Deut. 22. 5.

This being a Precept concerning natural Honefty, is of perpetual Equity. It is an univerfal Negative, and by Rules of Theology binds always, and therefore is now of force. This confounding of Garments has been ufed by Wantons, to favour their lafcivious Defigns. Thus *Theodora,* a *Roman* Matron, waited on *Stephanio* the Player, in Man's Apparel, as his Page. *Sueton. Oct.*

This was a Practice abominated by civilized Heathens. Nature has made difference not only between the Sex, but between the Apparel of Men and Women ; not only among the civilized, but barbarous Nations, that are vifibly diftinguifhed by the Diverfity of their Garments.

Whenever therefore this diftinguifhing Mark of the Sexes is gone, they have an Opportunity of converfing together with the moft unlimited Freedom ; and Shame, which is generally the greateft Obftacle to vicious Actions, having here no place, they greedily run into thofe Exceffes, which otherwife they durft fcarce have thought of. *Heliogabalus, Sporus, Sardanapalus, Caligula,* Priefts of *Venus,* and others who have ufed this Practice, are juftly branded in Hiftory as Monfters of Nature, the Scum, and Scandal, and Shame of Mankind.

If the Change of Drefs be thus deteftable among the Heathens, will they not rife up in Judgment againft thofe Chriftians who make it their common Practice, in thefe Mafquerades, and that with this profane View, that they might the more effectually cover their Villanies ?

This Practice has been alfo condemned by the Chriftian Church in all Ages.

TERTULLIAN says, That he finds no kind of Garment is cursed of God but Women's Apparel worn by Men, for such are an Abomination to God; that is, abhorred and cursed by him. What then will be judged of the Pantomime, the Stage-Player, who is attired in Womens Apparel?— *Quid de Pantomimo? De Spect. & Idol.*

CLEMENS ALEXANDRINUS looks upon it as a Breach of God's Law, which would not have Men to be effeminate.

CYPRIAN is of Opinion, that those, who wear Womens Apparel, are accursed, according to the Law.

EPIPHANIUS counts it shameful and dishonest for a Man to appear in the Form of a Woman. *Contr. Haeres. l. 2 & 3.*

I MIGHT add many more, and join the Councils, both former and latter, with them; but 'tis sufficient to let the Reader know, that the Christian Church has always condemned Mens putting on Womens Clothes, and Women Mens Clothes, as an infamous and scandalous Practice.

FROM the whole it appears, how the *Masquerading Practice* has been counted a Nusance, not only by Christians, but by Heathens; and that the Propagation and Continuance of it, has been entirely owing to the most corrupt Part of Mankind, those Excrescences of the human Nature.

IT is a Pastime utterly unlawful, being a *Congress to an unclean end*; not a Mystery of Iniquity, but an open Scene of outrageous and flaming Debauchery; where Temptation is passionately courted, the wanton Imagination indulged to the last degree, so that none who go there return from thence chaste and innocent. The most virtuous and resolute Mind is by degrees softened, and at last dissolved into Sensuality: These are the common and sad Effects of the amorous Intrigues, and those luscious Indecencies (heightened by the Enchantments of Musick) usually practised by Masqueraders.

I WILL close the whole, with this Dilemma to the masquerading Ladies:

EITHER *you are pleased with the Indecencies and Obscenities of the Masquerades, or you are not.*

IF *you are pleased with them*, you are pleased with open Lewdness (that Entertainment being confessedly so) which is too gross a Reflection upon your Virtue, and upon that

F   sacred

facred Regard your Sex always (at leaft above ours) paid
to the Laws of Decency, and Forms of Breeding, as well
as to the Maxims of Religion. Thus the Gentleman,
who thinks it no Crime to fwear, counts it Rudenefs
to do fo in the Prefence of the Ladies, as prefuming it
will be more grating in their Ears, than thofe of his own
Sex.

IF *you are not pleafed with thofe Obfcenities,* why do you
go there, and, by your Company and Purfe, encourage
them? Why will you attend thofe Diverfions, where the
Monfter of Vice is reprefented in its full Proportion, and
where all Impreffions of Virtue and Sacred Things are per-
fectly effaced and expunged.

Now therefore to frequent thefe Plays, what is it but to
compliment Vice, which, in Mr. *Collier's* Opinion, *is but one
Remove from worfhipping the Devil. Preface to the Short View,*
ad finem.

LET therefore Motives of Honour, Decency, and Virtue
keep you within the bounds of Home; and if you would
preferve the Health of your Soul, *go no more to the Peft-
houfe for Recreation.*

LUDOVICUS VIVES (who lived in K. *Henry* the VIIIth's
time, and was Tutor to the Princefs *Mary,* afterwards
Queen of *England*) relates, That a ftrong Town debauched,
was heretofore reformed by the Beauty of Women, who,
ferioufly addicted themfelves to Virtue, and never beheld
any Man with a good Will (who required them in Marriage)
that had not firft ranged himfelf in the Lifts of Devotion
and Piety.

To conclude, in the words of the Bifhop of *Arras,* in
his Order againft Plays, *Decemb.* 4. *A. D.* 1697. where he
fays, ' A Man muft be very ignorant of his Religion not to
' know the great Difguft (*l' Horreur*) it has always declared
' for publick Sights, and for Plays in particular; the holy
' Fathers condemn it in their Writings, looking on them as
' Relicks of Heathenifm, and Schools of Debauchery.'
' They have been always abominated by the Church, the
' Rituals of the beft governed Dioceffes have ranged the
' Players among excommunicated Perfons: The *Ritual* of
' *Paris* joins them with Sorcerers and Magicians; the moft
' eminent Bifhops have publickly deny'd them the Sacra-
' ments,

ments, others have refused to bury them in confecrated Ground.'

UNLESS therefore we have a mind to condemn the Church, the holy Fathers, and the moft holy Bifhops, 'tis impoffible to juftify Plays.'

F I N I S.

BOOKS Printed for EMAN. MATTHEWS, *at the*
Bible *in* Pater-noster-Row.

1. THE Validity of the Diſſenting Miniſtry. In Four Parts.
2. Plain-Dealing ; or Separation without Schiſm, and
Schiſm without Separation. The Seventh Edition. Pr. 6 d.
Theſe two by the Reverend Mr. *Charles Owen.*

A Vindication of Plain-Dealing, &c. The Second Edition. Price 4 d.

Plain-Dealing, and its Vindication defended. Price 6 d.

The Chriſtian Philoſopher. By the Reverend *Cotton Ma-
ther,* D. D.

An Eſſay on Health. By the Reverend Mr. *B. Groſvenor,*

The Art of Reading and Writing *Engliſh.* By the Reverend Mr. *J. Watts.*

The Pſalms of *David* in Metre. By the Reverend Dr.
John Patrick.

Hymns and Spiritual Songs. By the Reverend Mr. *Simon
Browne.*

The Occaſional Papers. In three Volumes. Being Eſſays
on various Subjeéts and Occaſions.

A Defence of the Scripture, as the only Standard of Faith,
&c. By the Author of the Occaſional Paper. Price 2 s.

Memoirs of the Church of *Scotland.* In four Periods.

The Family-Inſtruétor. In two Volumes. The Ninth
Edition.

In a few Days will be Publiſh'd,

1. A Brief, Praétical, and Pacifick Diſcourſe of God, and
of Father, Son, and Spirit, and of our Concern with
them. With an Appendix. By the Reverend *Joſhua Old-
field,* D. D. The Second Edition. Price 1 s.

2. Liberty without Libertiniſm ; or, a Diſcourſe, to evince
the Reaſonableneſs of every Chriſtian's judging for himſelf
in Religious Matters. By a Well-wiſher to Truth and Liberty. Price 1 s.

3. A Layman's Plain Remarks on a Fine Diſcourſe of a
Nameleſs Author, intitled, *The Church of* England *free
from the Imputation of Popery.* Price 6 d.

E 0